THE GERMAN STATES
AT THE TIME OF THE REFORMATION

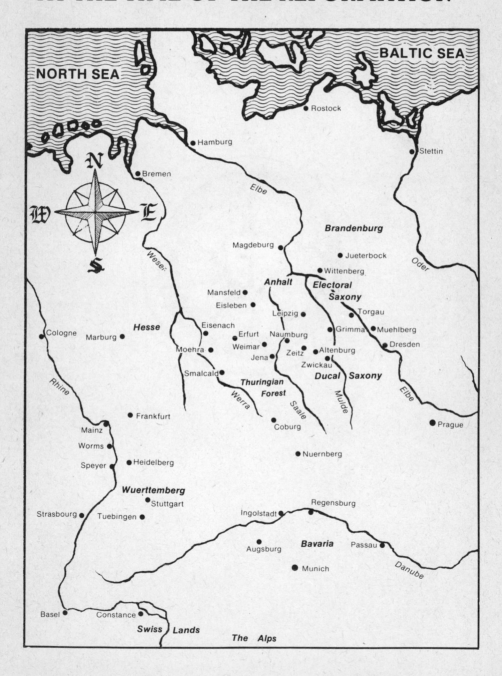

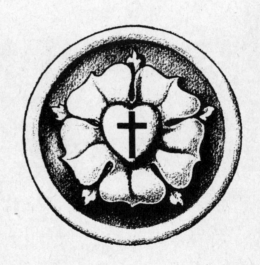

THE
Life and Faith
OF
Martin Luther

ADOLPH FEHLAUER

Illustrations by
Steven D. MacLeod

NORTHWESTERN PUBLISHING HOUSE
Milwaukee, Wisconsin

Library of Congress Catalog Card Number 80-84134
Northwestern Publishing House
3624 West North Ave., Milwaukee, Wis. 53208
© 1981 by Northwestern Publishing House. All rights reserved.
Published 1981
Printed in the United States of America

ISBN 0-8100-0125-X

CONTENTS

INTRODUCTION

The year is 1517. It is the day before All Saints Day, an important church festival for all devout Catholics. But something besides All Saints Day is on the minds of many people in Wittenberg, Germany. On the streets and in the shops townspeople and students are excitedly discussing something that interests and troubles them very much. As they talk, some of them point to papers they have in their hands. Let us listen in on one of the groups.

"Where did you get that letter of indulgence?"

"From a priest called John Tetzel. He is selling them in Jueterbock. Tetzel says that God will not punish anyone who buys an indulgence letter like this. He will not have to go to purgatory when he dies."

"You better tell Dr. Luther about that paper and what John Tetzel is doing. I don't think that Dr. Luther will approve of it. And I'm sure that he will not like what you did. Don't you remember that he preached a very strong sermon against the misuse of indulgences last February? Some students also told me that Luther knows what Tetzel is up to and that he is going to do something about it. Look, there is Luther now."

They look up and see Luther walking down the steps of the Augustinian Cloister. In one hand he has a large sheet of paper, in the other a hammer. He walks resolutely down the path toward the Market Place. As he passes by the students and other groups of people, he greets them cordially but does not pause to visit with them as is his usual custom. His mind is occupied with what is written on the paper and with what he is about to do. His destination is the Castle Church. After a fifteen minute walk, he reaches the main door on the north side of the building. Without hesitation he holds the sheet of paper up, and with a few hammer blows nails it to the Castle Church door.

There was really nothing that seemed unusual in what Martin Luther had done. The church door was often used as a bulletin board for notices and news items. Nor did Luther think that what he had written would arouse more than the usual interest. His message was a list of 95 theses, or statements. In them he expressed his opinion about the sale of indulgences and the forgiveness of sins. In the introduction, he invited his fellow professors and others to debate the theses with him.

Little did Luther realize that his actions on October 31, 1517 would mark the beginning of a great reformation of the church and of the return of the pure word of God to the people of the world.

I

THE TIME
IN WHICH LUTHER LIVED

Martin Luther lived at a time when many important changes were taking place in the world, especially in Europe. It was also a time of strife and confusion. All this influenced and affected Luther's life and work. Before we begin our study of Luther's life it is important that we become somewhat acquainted with conditions that existed in Luther's homeland, Germany, and with the changes that were taking place at that time.

A Divided Germany

At Luther's time Germany consisted of more than 300 separate territories and estates, some quite large, others very small. There was no central German government, no united Germany. Some of the areas were governed by princes, some by bishops of the Catholic Church, and many smaller parts, consisting of a few acres with a castle, were under the control of knights. All the states and areas in Germany were actually part of the Holy Roman Empire, but the emperor at Luther's time exercised little authority over most of them. In fact, German princes practically ruled their territories as they pleased. If a prince decided not to cooperate with the emperor, there was little the emperor could do about it.

The Authority of the Pope

For many years the most influential ruling organization was not the secular or state government but the Roman Catholic Church. Over a period of years it had become very wealthy and powerful. The individual churches and all the priests, bishops and common people were under the leadership and control of the pope in Rome. He claimed that he was the vicar of Christ and God's representative on earth and that he was the supreme ruler in both the church and the state. Not only churches and their priests and bishops were to obey him, but he also claimed authority over the political states and their princes and emperors. This resulted in almost constant strife between the pope and the political rulers.

Great pressure was often exerted upon those who did not obey the decrees of the pope and of the Catholic Church. For example, Emperor Henry IV insisted that the territory over which he was ruler belonged to him and not to the church and that he could do with his land as he wished. Pope Gregory VII then put the whole empire of Henry IV under the interdict. That meant that all churches in the empire would be closed and no one could receive the blessings of the church as long as the interdict was in force. This decree of the pope forced Henry IV to come to the castle where the pope was staying and beg him to cancel the interdict. But the pope refused even to see him when he first appeared. It was mid-winter, and the emperor was forced to stand in the snow for three days before he was allowed to enter the castle. He then fell on his knees before the pope and asked for forgiveness. The interdict was cancelled, and the emperor was again in the good graces of the pope.

The popes felt that they were supreme in all spiritual matters and that they possessed the keys to heaven. Obedience to the pope was considered necessary for salvation. Anyone who did not obey the pope was excommunicated. That meant that he could not partake of the sacraments of the church, and his property was taken away from him. Anyone who disagreed with the teachings of the church was branded a heretic and was in grave danger of being put under the ban, cruelly punished, and even put to death. Secret trials were often held where the accused were tortured in order to make them confess that they were in error.

False Teachings of the Church

Since there was no strong central government in Germany, the pope was able to tax the people as he pleased. Many kinds of taxes and fees were collected by the priests and bishops to fill the treasury of the church. The people had to pay for almost everything the church had to offer, even the sacraments. As the church grew greedier, wealthier, and more powerful, it became more and more interested in the things and honors of this world. As a result, it did little to help the people with their spiritual needs. The church had actually lost and forgotten its true purpose. The bishops and priests woefully neglected the teaching and preaching of God's Word. False teachings and practices, even superstition, had taken the place of the gospel of salvation through faith in Jesus Christ. The pope decided what the bishops, priests, and monks were to teach and preach, and the people usually accepted without question what they were told. For example, they were told that Jesus was a stern, angry judge, and not the merciful Savior from sin as we know him from the Bible. People who were troubled about their sins were told to make amends and gain favor with God by doing good works, praying to the saints, and making pilgrimages to shrines that supposedly contained relics and bodies of saints. The people were told to pray to various saints instead of to Jesus. St. Lupus protected against wolves; St. Clarus cured toothaches; St. Agatha prevented earthquakes. The Virgin Mary was the most popular saint. The people called upon her to pray before the throne of God to relieve them from their sins and troubles.

The Catholic Church taught that the traditions of the church, the teachings of the church fathers, and the pronouncements of the pope were supreme, not the Scriptures. A decree of the church in 1223 stated that lay people dare not own a Bible. Only priests could have Latin copies of the Bible. Those who owned translations of the Bible were to give them to their bishop, who was to burn them. The people and priests were told that only the Catholic Church, in particular the pope, could explain the Scriptures correctly.

The people believed that by doing what the church asked them to do and by living pious lives they could obtain favor with God and eternal salvation. To escape from the temptations of the wicked world, men and women often entered monasteries and cloisters. There they would spend their time in fasting, praying, studying , and working. In that way they thought they could make themselves acceptable to God.

Corruption in the Church

The most important activity of the priest was to administer the seven sacraments of the Catholic Church. The sacraments of the Mass and penance were of special significance. The church taught that by the reading of the Mass the priest was able to change the bread and wine in the Lord's Supper into the body and blood of Jesus Christ. It also taught that the a sacrifice of Jesus was repeated all over again at every Mass. According to the sacrament of penance, the people were to confess their sins to the priest and to show evidence that they truly were sorry for their sins. They had to prove their sorrow by carrying out certain penalties that were ordered by the priest, such as making pilgrimages, doing some humble services, praying, or paying a certain amount of money to the church. The pardon that the priest then issued was called an indulgence. In the minds of the people the indulgence meant payment to God for the forgivenesss of their sins and for the time they would otherwise have to spend in purgatory. In Roman Catholic teaching, purgatory is a place of suffering between heaven and hell.

The corruptness of the church could also be seen in the way the priests, bishops and popes lived and carried out their work. The priests often were uneducated. Some were not even able to read the liturgy in the church services. Many became so negligent and lazy that they didn't even bother to hear confessions or to read the Mass. There were exceptions. A few priests were conscientious and led pious lives, but many of them were greedy, lazy, and immoral. They devoted most of their time to collecting money for the treasury of the pope in Rome.

The Troubled Christians

When we realize the greed, worldliness, false teachings, and unscriptural practices of the church, we can understand why the common people and sincere churchmen became very much concerned and troubled. More and more of them began to ask: How long can this continue? But changes were taking place, especially in Germany. There general education was increasing. Universities were being established in many major cities. In Germany alone nine universities were started between 1450 and 1517. Mining and trades were increasing. New and better means of communication and travel were developing. Living conditions of the common people improved as salaries increased. Princes likewise became wealthier and more powerful. The princes made known their resentment over the fact that the church owned and controlled large estates. They were also greatly disturbed by the heavy taxes the church imposed on them and by its methods of getting money from the people.

The common people were becoming disturbed and disgruntled. They had to work hard and pay endless taxes to the church. But they received very few spiritual benefits from the church, while the priests, bishops and pope lived in luxury. They did not find true spiritual satisfaction by making pilgrimages and attending Latin church services that they could not understand. They wanted help and comfort for their souls and spiritual guidance for their lives, but the church was not giving that to them. Many longed for the return of God's Word. They hoped and prayed for a reformer.

Luther's Forerunners

Several brave and consecrated men attempted to bring about reforms in the church. Two of them were John Wycliffe (1325-1384) in England and John Huss (1369-1415) in Bohemia.

Wycliffe criticized the church for letting the priests neglect their work and live a life of ease and luxury. He tried very hard to get the church to permit the people to read the Bible, but he did not succeed. The church declared Wycliffe a heretic. In spite of great opposition, he succeeded in translating the Bible into the English language. Forty-one years after his death they dug up his remains and burned them as well as copies of all his books.

John Huss believed and taught that the Scriptures are superior to the pronouncements of the pope. He also attacked the church for permitting the negligent and immoral priests to continue as servants of the church. He was condemned as a heretic and burned at the stake. As he came to the place where he was to die, he prayed, "Lord Jesus Christ, I will bear patiently and humbly this horrible, shameful, and cruel death for the sake of the gospel and the preaching of the Word."

Wycliffe and Huss failed in their attempts to reform a corrupt church and to restore the gospel. But perhaps their words, works and examples would help someone else in another time.

II

THE
PEASANT'S SON

God heard the cry of his people. On November 10, 1483 a son was born to Hans and Margaret Luther. He was the one chosen by God to lead his people out of their spiritual slavery. Just as God had prepared Moses to lead the Children of Israel out of the Egyptian slavery into the Promised Land, so the Lord now would prepare a leader to lead his people out of the bondage of misbelief and superstition to the saving gospel of Jesus Christ.

Faithful Catholics and Good Parents

Hans and Margaret Luther were faithful members of St. Peter's Catholic Church in Eisleben, Germany. Already on the day after their son was born they had him baptized by the local priest. Since November 11th was St. Martin's Day, they named him Martin.

Hans and Margaret Luther had come to Eisleben from Moehra, a small town on the edge of the Thuringian Forest in Saxony. There Hans grew to manhood and farmed with his father and brothers. Since it was the custom that the youngest son in the family always inherited the farm, Hans left his home in Moehra and moved to Eisleben where he found work in the copper mines. The work in the mines was hard and the salary poor, so one year later he decided to move his family to Mansfeld, five miles northwest of Eisleben. Martin was six months old at the time. There Hans continued to work in the mines. Although he grew up on a farm, he spent most of his life working in the mines. That is why Martin Luther later referred to himself as both a miner's and peasant's son. He said, "I am a peasant's son. My father, grandfather, and all my ancestors were real peasants."

Martin's parents were hard-working and thrifty. They had to be to support their family of seven children. Martin Luther himself once said, "My father was a poor miner, and my mother carried wood from the forest on her back. They both worked their flesh off their backs in order to bring up their children." What Luther said about his parents could be said about most of the common people, the peasants; they all had to struggle to make a living. His father was ambitious and dependable, so gradually his position and income improved. In time he was even able to lease and operate some smelting furnaces and to buy his own home.

It was in Mansfeld that Martin spent his childhood. Parents at that time did not believe that children should be pampered. They were strict and demanded respect and obedience from their children. Sometimes the punishment was overly severe. Later in one of his table talks Luther said, "My father flogged me so severely one day that I ran away and had a grudge against him. On account of a nut I had stolen, my mother once beat me till the blood flowed." But such harsh punishment was evidently unusual in the Luther household, for Luther often stated that his father was of a cheerful nature and that his mother regularly sang with the children. Martin knew that his parents meant well. They felt their responsibility as parents and did not want to fail in giving their children a good training. Luther loved his parents and honored them to the end of his life.

A Religion of Fear

Religion was very important to the people in Germany, and also in the Luther home. Luther's parents attended Mass regularly, and prayers were said mornings and evenings and at mealtime. They tried hard to instill in their children a fear of God and a devotion for the Catholic Church. But Martin's parents did not teach him to know God as a loving Father who sent Jesus to earth as his Savior. He was taught to regard Jesus as a stern, angry judge who could be kept from punishing people only if they asked Mary to help them and to pray for them. Fear filled his heart when he thought about Jesus or saw pictures of him. He said, "From early childhood I turned pale and trembled whenever I heard the name of Christ. I was taught that we ourselves had to atone for our sins." The common people of Germany were very superstitious. Martin's parents told him that goblins, elves, and demons lived in the neighborhood forests and that they were responsible for fires, sicknesses, accidents, and many other misfortunes.

Although Martin's parents meant it well, unknowingly they had given him a wrong concept of God and of God's plan of salvation. The training he received at home and by the church did not instill confidence, joy, and hope, but a superstitious fear. Many years later Martin Luther would find the joy and peace that only God can give through his holy Word.

III

THE
SCHOOLBOY

Martin Luther was only four-and-a-half years old when his father enrolled him in the local elementary school. Why at such an early age? Hans and Margaret Luther must have felt that their son was ready for school, and most likely Martin was eager to join the children who passed by his house on their way to school. He also had available an unusual kind of free transportation. An older student, Nicolaus Oemler, often carried little Martin to school on his shoulders whenever the roads were muddy or covered with deep snow.

Elementary School in Mansfeld

Today children frequently enter kindergarten at the age of four or five, but the school in Mansfeld had no kindergarten class for the beginners. It was a Latin school. Latin was the most important subject. It was the language that was generally used by the teachers in teaching also the other subjects. Although German was spoken in the homes, in school students were expected to use Latin in their conversations as soon as possible. At that time Latin was the language of all educated people. By the time Martin reached the sixth grade he could speak and write Latin quite well. The purpose of much of the instruction was to make the children good Catholics. They were required to memorize the sections of the Bible read in the church services, the Creed, the Lord's Prayer, the confession of sins, the Commandments, and the Hail Mary. Other subjects taught were reading, writing, arithmetic, and music. Singing was considered to be very important. The students were especially drilled in singing the liturgy so they could participate in the various church services. Older children had to serve as choir boys.

John Gutenberg had recently invented the printing press, but very few school books were available, and students seldom could afford to purchase those that were. The children had to learn by drill and repetition. Facts were repeated over and over again until they were literally pounded into the children's heads. Most of the children did their writing on slates or on the chalkboard. Only older students were permitted to use paper and pens.

Discipline was strict, and children were expected to work hard at their studies both at home and in school. Parents were told that if they did not permit the teacher to discipline their children in the way he though most effective, they could not enroll them in school. Children were punished in various ways for misbehavior and for unacceptable recitations. The teachers were strict, and at times harsh. But this was expected by both parents and pupils. Luther was a gifted boy and usually learned his lessons well, but one day he received fifteen strokes with the rod because he had not learned his Latin assignments well enough. It is quite possible that the fifteen strokes were punishment for a week's accumulation of unsatisfactory recitations. Even though his teachers were strict and demanding, Martin respected them. And his parents were grateful for the instruction and training their son received from them.

High School in Magdeburg

When Martin was fourteen years old, his father enrolled him in the high school in Magdeburg. This school was conducted by a society called the Brethren of the Common Life. It had a good reputation, and Hans wanted his children to receive the best education possible. He had recently acquired part control of several smelters; therefore he was able to send his son to this boarding school.

Magdeburg, a city of twelve-thousand people, was sixty miles from Martin's home. The city was filled with Catholic churches and chapels. There were reminders everywhere that this was a religious community. There were crosses and shrines along the roadways; priests, monks, and nuns walking about; the ringing of bells at regular intervals; and almost daily religious street processions. Luther also saw many poor people and beggars. He saw one begging monk who had once been the wealthy and famous Count William von Anhalt. This monk made a deep and lasting impression on him and had much to do with a decision that he later made. Luther later described the incident: "I saw with my own eyes a prince of Anhalt who went in a friar's cowl on the highway to beg bread. Like a donkey he carried a sack which was so heavy that he bent under it, while his companion walked by his side without a burden. This prince alone might serve as an example of the grizzly, shorn holiness of the world. They had so cowed him that he did all the works of the cloister like any other brother, and he had so fasted, watched, and mortified his flesh that he looked like a death's-head, mere skin and bones; indeed, he soon after died, for he could not long bear to live such a severe life. In short, whoever looked at him had to gasp for pity and must needs be ashamed of his own worldly occupation."

Luther diligently applied himself to his studies, but he also joined with the other students in having fun. Since he enjoyed music, he joined a singing group that sang three- and four-part songs for their own enjoyment and for the enjoyment of the townspeople. Occasionally they would

stop to sing in front of homes and then ask for "hand-outs."
Later Luther told about an experience he and his friends
had as they sang in front of a farmer's house: "As we were
wandering through the town singing from house to house,
we stopped at a farmer's house at the end of the village.
Soon the farmer came out and shouted in a harsh voice,
'Boys, where are you?' We thought he was angry that we
had disturbed him and ran off as fast as we could. When we
stopped and looked back, we saw that he had a sausage and
other food in his hands. We quickly returned and gratefully
took the food he kindly offered us."

It is very likely that Luther saw the complete Bible for the
first time while he was attending the school in Magdeburg.
It was while he was examining various books in the library
that he came upon a Latin Bible. He eagerly paged through
the huge volume which was chained to a table. He was
amazed that the Bible contained much more than was read
or referred to in school or in the church services. He stopped
at the story of Samuel and his mother Hannah. He read the
entire section with great interest. From then on it was his
one great desire to always have access to a complete Bible
and possibly to own one. But Bibles were very expensive
and were therefore usually found only in some libraries and
in the homes of a few rich people. Very few priests owned
complete Bibles.

High School in Eisenach

Only during the rare vacations did Martin and a good
friend, John Reinicke, get back to their homes in Mansfeld.
In those days most people traveled on foot, and sixty miles
was a long way from home for a fifteen-year-old boy. Hans
and Margaret were concerned because their son did not
have someone closer to look after him, especially if he
should become ill. Martin's mother had relatives in Eisenach. If he enrolled in school there, possibly they would
provide lodging and meals for him. So after only one year at
Magdeburg, Martin was transferred to St. George's School

in Eisenach, twenty-five miles farther away from home. Unfortunately he could not find lodging with relatives as his parents had hoped. For a time he lived in one of the infirmaries, or dormitories, of the school.

Eisenach was a city of about two-thousand people. On a high hill overlooking the city stood a famous old castle, the Wartburg. Luther himself would add to the fame of that castle when in 1521 it would serve as a place of refuge for him. Below the castle was a small monastery that was founded and supported by the wealthy Schwalbe family of Eisenach.

Martin's father had big plans for his son's future. He wanted him to become one of the best lawyers in Germany. That is why he sacrificed in order to send him to the best schools in Germany. The four years at St. George's School were to prepare him for entrance to a university. Martin applied himself diligently to his work. He excelled in most of his studies and became very proficient in writing and speaking Latin. He did especially well in writing essays and in public speaking.

At Eisenach Luther had the privilege of studying under some very able teachers. One of his favorite instructors was John Trebonius. He had the habit of doffing his cap when he entered the classroom. He said, "I treat my students with respect. God will one day make some of these boys mayors, chancellors, doctors, and magistrates." One day a famous professor from the university of Erfurt visited St. George's School. Martin Luther was selected to prepare and deliver the welcoming speech. Doctor Trutvetter, the visiting professor, was pleased with the address, and Martin made a good impression on the visitor. Before the professor left, he said to Trebonius: "Keep an eye on that Luther. There is something in that boy. By all means prepare him for the university and send him to me at Erfurt." To Martin he said, "My son, the Lord has bestowed special gifts on you. Use them faithfully in his service. When you are ready and wish to come to Erfurt, remember that you have a good friend there — Doctor Trutvetter. He will give you a friendly reception."

Martin Luther's years in Eisenach were happy ones. The one thing that added greatly to his happiness was the kindness shown him by two families — the Schwalbes and the Cottas. They often helped and befriended students who attended St. George's School. Mrs. Cotta learned to know Luther well, and she was impressed with his fine Christian attitude and his singing in the church choir. She invited him to have his meals at her home. The Schwalbes were relatives of the Cotta family. They asked Luther to help their son Henry with his studies in return for free lodging. To this Luther heartily agreed. Both families were very devout, and they were faithful members of the church. Their strong religious conviction greatly influenced Luther. The vicar of the local monastery was a frequent visitor at the Schwalbe home, and Martin had many serious conversations with him. The Cottas and Schwalbes made Luther's school days in Eisenach very pleasant and interesting. He came in contact with good music and good books, and he became acquainted with many influential and interesting people. Later in life Luther often said that his years in Eisenach were the happiest ones in his life. He called Eisenach "my beloved city."

In that beloved city he had found good teachers, good friends, and a home-away-from-home, but he still had not found the God-given way to eternal salvation. To him Jesus still was only the stern judge and not the loving Savior.

IV

THE
UNIVERSITY STUDENT

By the age of seventeen Luther had completed the required courses for enrollment in a university. His father was determined that Martin should now prepare himself to study law and become a lawyer. But man's thoughts and plans are not always God's thoughts and plans. Several events that occurred during Luther's college days completely changed the direction of his life. A freak accident, the sudden death of a fellow student, and a severe thunder storm affected him in such a way that he never carried out his father's wish to become a lawyer.

Life and Studies at the University

Attending a university was costly, but Luther's parents decided that they would do without many things in their home so that their son could receive a good education. The Leipzig university was close to Mansfeld, but the university at Erfurt had a better reputation. So in May 1501 Martin entered the Erfurt University, which had an enrollment of about 2,000 students.

The city of Erfurt had a population of 20,000 people. It was the largest city that Luther had ever seen. Martin was impressed with the many kinds of business places and the constant activities in the stores and on the streets. Luther was also impressed with the many Catholic churches, chapels, hospitals, and monasteries. His four years in Erfurt gave him many opportunities to get acquainted with the business and social life of the city and to participate in its many religious pageants and celebrations.

Luther lived in a dormitory near the university. Dormitory rules and regulations were exacting and strictly enforced. In order to make the best use of daylight all students had to get up at four o'clock in the morning and be in bed by eight o'clock in the evening. They had to wear certain prescribed clothes for different occasions. Permission had to be granted before a student could leave the dormitory after closing hours. Every student was expected to make regular private confessions to his priest. But there was also time for fun. Martin Luther enjoyed the company of his fellow students, and he spent many happy hours with them playing games, hiking in the hills near Erfurt, and singing student songs.

Before Martin could begin his law studies he had to complete the undergraduate course. He applied himself very diligently to his studies although he was not very much interested in some of the subjects that he had to take. His teachers commended him for his good work, and his classmates respected him. They nicknamed him "the philosopher" because he was especially gifted in argumentation and debating. Already in 1502 he received his Bachelor of Arts degree, and in 1505 he was awarded the Master's Degree. He ranked second in a class of seventeen students.

Two Accidents

Luther usually went home to Mansfeld during college vacations. On a return trip after an Easter holiday at home he had an accident that made him think very seriously about his soul's welfare and life after death. He and a friend were only a short distance from Erfurt when Martin accidentally cut his upper leg with the dagger he was carrying at his side. No matter what they tried, the bleeding would not stop. His friend ran for help. Martin lay on his back and tried to stop the bleeding by pressing down on the wound. This caused the leg to swell and pain severely. In his fear he called on the Virgin Mary to spare his life. Friends came and helped him to the University dormitory. That night the wound started to bleed again. The doctor feared for his life. Again and again Martin prayed to Mary for help. After some time the wound healed, and Martin regained his strength. But he was greatly distressed for many days. Afterwards he said, "If I had died then, I should have placed my hope of salvation in the Virgin Mary." While recovering from the wound, he occupied himself by learning to play the lute. When he returned to classes he surprised his friends with his new skill. Later in life he made good use of that skill in composing new hymns for the home and church.

On another occasion Martin was greatly distressed by the sudden, violent death of a friend. He imagined himself in his place and seriously wondered, "Where would my soul now be if it were I who had been killed?"

A Troubled Soul

Martin never had been enthusiastic about becoming a lawyer. Now, after these experiences, his soul's welfare became his greatest concern. He never had forgotten the ragged former prince he saw begging in the streets of Magdeburg. When he thought of him, he felt ashamed that he was doing so little to please God. Martin thought that, instead of pleasing God, he was displeasing him and adding more and more sins to his soul and more and more years of punishment in purgatory. In spite of all his leaning, he had not found the answer to the question, "How can I become truly acceptable to God?" He had learned that

Jesus suffered and died for the sins of the world, but he had not learned that forgiveness is a free gift of God and that Jesus had truly died for him. He was taught that God's wrath could only be appeased by good works and through the prayers of the saints. The more he thought about his relation to God, the more he was convinced that he should do what the prince von Anhalt had done — forsake the world and become a monk in a monastery. By doing that, he thought, he could make sure his eternal salvation.

After completing his studies for his master's degree in 1505, Luther spent several weeks with his parents in Mansfeld. On the last day of vacation his father surprised him by giving him a complete set of law books. Martin thanked his father for those costly books for which he had labored and saved for a long time. How could he now tell his parents that he was not at all sure that he wanted to study law and that he had thoughts of becoming a monk!

The Vow to Become a Monk

On the way back to Erfurt a sudden thunder storm came up. Luther found shelter under a tree. Suddenly a bolt of lightning struck near him and knocked him to the ground. In terror he cried out, "Save me, St. Anne. I will become a monk!" As he continued his journey, he was troubled by the vow he had made. Many questions entered his mind. Was the bolt of lightning a sign of God's wrath toward him? How could he tell his father that he had made a vow to become a monk? What would he say? He did not know whether he had done the right thing or not, but he believed that a vow once made must be kept.

After Luther's return to the university, he sold most of his books and made other preparations to leave. He knew he had to inform his father of his decision to become a monk. This would be very difficult to do. His father, who had sacrificed so much to give him a good education, would be deeply hurt. His visions of Martin becoming a great lawyer would suddenly disappear. Worst of all, his son would be discontinuing his studies in order to become a monk, and Martin knew that his father had little good to say about monks. Hans Luther felt that they led useless lives and lived off of hard-working people by their begging. These thoughts ran through Martin's mind as he was about to write to his father. Martin knew his father would be very disappointed and angry, but he strongly felt that his vow to St. Anne must be kept. In great agony he wrote to his father, begging him please to understand why he had to live up to the vow he had made.

On the evening of July 16, 1505 Luther invited his college friends to a party. Everyone enjoyed himself. At the end of the evening Luther shocked his friends by telling them of the vow he had made and of his decision to enter the Augustinian Monastery in Erfurt. He said, "Today you see me and then never again." They tried to make him change his mind, but their efforts were useless. The next day they sadly accompaned him to the Augustinian Monastery on the outskirts of the city. After a tearful farewell, Luther walked through the gate of the monastery. A highly gifted Master of Arts was about to become a monk. But this was also a part of God's plan in preparing Luther for the great work that he was to do in God's kingdom on earth.

V

THE
MONK

Martin Luther entered the monastery with the firm belief that as a monk he could attain perfection and thus make sure his eternal salvation. There he thought he would be secure against temptations and be able to live a truly God-pleasing life. But did Luther find peace of mind and achieve the joy of perfection in the monastery? Hardly. Later in life he said, "For twenty years I was always sad. I must have been the most miserable creature on earth."

The Conscientious Monk

During the first year in the monastery Martin Luther had to serve as a novice. It was a year of probation, or testing, in which he had to prove that he was worthy of becoming a monk. He was given a long white robe and a black mantle. His hair was clipped and the top of his head was shaved. His small unheated cell was furnished with only a table, a chair, and a straw bed. Luther was instructed to avoid unnecessary talk and to walk quietly with his head bowed low. He was assigned many tasks which he conscientiously carried out. At daybreak a bell would ring to awaken the monks. Each day consisted of prayer, study, and manual work. All monks had to attend seven prayer sessions in the chapel every day. In between they had to carry out their assigned tasks. There was little time for rest.

After Luther had completed his year as a novice, he was ready to take the oath and to become a monk. At the cloister altar he swore that he would be loyal to the Augustinian Order and to God as long as he would live. He was now told to study for the priesthood. This gave him the opportunity to study the Latin Bible. He also spent much time in studying Hebrew and Greek, the languages in which the Bible was originally written.

In 1507 Martin Luther was ordained to the priesthood. This was an honor that not many monks received. The ordination was a very special occasion. Monks had the right to invite relatives and friends to be present at the ordination. Luther invited his parents, and he was pleasantly surprised when his father came and even made a donation to the monastery. This was the first time that father and son had met since Martin entered the monastery. Although Luther's father came to the ordination, he was not convinced that his son had done the right thing when he decided to give up his law studies to become a monk. After the ordination he said to Martin, "You are a learned scholar. Haven't you ever read in the Scriptures that you should honor your father and mother?"

As a priest Luther could now read the Mass, the most important sacrament of the church. In that sacrament the priest supposedly performs a miracle. The church taught that as the priest blessed the bread and wine, those elements turned into the body and blood of Christ. Luther was filled with terror as he spoke the words, "We offer unto thee, the living, the true, the eternal God." How could he, a sinful being, address the holy God? How could he stand in the very presence of the body and blood of Christ? He knew he was a sinner, and unacceptable to God. How could he then stand before God who demanded holiness!

The Troubled Monk

Even though Luther kept all the rules and regulations of the monastery, and even did much more than was required, he still had doubts about his salvation. At the age of 23 he felt that he still was not at peace with his God. He anxiously sought peace for his soul. He faithfully repeated the Lord's Prayer and Ave Maria over and over again. He did all the "good works" that were required of monks and added some of his own. Sometimes he went without food for days. He beat himself until the blood came. He slept without covers on the stone floor of his unheated cell. "I was a pious monk," he wrote later. "I kept the rules of the monastery more strictly than I can tell. If ever a monk could have gone to heaven by observing the rules of a cloister, I should have been that one. If I had kept on much longer with prayers, sleepless nights, work, reading, and abuses to my body, I would have killed myself."

Luther had done everything he could possibly think of to please and appease God, but he still did not feel that he was acceptable to God, who demanded holiness and who said, "Walk before me and be thou perfect." One day when he was greatly depressed, John Staupitz, the vicar general of the Augustinian order, came to him to console him. He said to him, "Why do you torment yourself with such doubts and fears? Look to Jesus Christ. He shed his blood for you. Trust in him and in the salvation he has earned for you. Another piece of advice — study the Bible." Luther did not grasp the full meaning of what Dr. Staupitz told him but later he said, "If the good doctor had not given me some hope in my agony, I should have despaired completely."

In 1508 Martin Luther received a letter from Dr. Staupitz which read, "At the request of the rector of Wittenberg University and upon the invitation of Prince Frederick, you are appointed to teach logic and ethics at the new university in Wittenberg." Luther obediently accepted the appointment. For about a year he served on the Wittenberg faculty. His living quarters were in the Black Cloister. There he was able to study and to meditate on God's Word. In 1509 he was asked to return to the Erfurt University.

The Disillusioned Monk

Martin Luther was a dedicated member of the Catholic Church. He fully accepted its teachings and practices, but he was troubled that all his efforts to abide by the requirements of the church had not made him sure of his salvation. Many questions continually came to his mind: Is man really able to save himself? Are monastery rules and regulations from God or from man? Are the writings of the church fathers superior to the Scriptures? A visit to Rome, the capitol and "holy city" of the Catholic Church, made matters worse for him. What he saw and heard there added more questions to his troubled mind and increased his doubts.

In November 1510 John Staupitz had asked Luther and another monk to go to Rome as representatives of the Augustinian monasteries in Germany. A strife had developed between two groups in the Augustinian Order. Luther and a fellow monk, John von Micheln, were to go to Rome and present the matter to the officials of the church for settlement. Luther was overjoyed that he was chosen to make the journey to the holy city. He had never hoped for such an honor and for the privilege of seeing the home of the pope and all the holy places. It was a long hard journey of eight-hundred-fifty miles. The two monks were often exhausted and footsore. Fortunately there were monasteries along the way where they found lodging. As they traveled they met many pilgrims who were on the way to or from the holy city. After twelve weeks of walking, Luther and his friend had crossed the Alps and Appennine Mountains. Before them was the Tiber River and the holy city of Rome! The twenty-seven-year-old Luther was overcome with emotion. He fell on his knees and cried out, "Hail thou holy Rome!" There before him sprawled the city in which Peter and Paul and the martyrs had lived and died. Their bodies

"If ever a monk could have gone to heaven by observing the rules of a cloister, I should have been that one."

lay buried in the shrines of the city. Above all, this was the home of the holy Father, Pope Julius II and his cardinals.

After some delay, Luther and his companion presented the matter regarding the Augustinian dispute to the proper officials of the church. They met with them several times, but only after four weeks did they reach a conclusion in the matter. Luther therefore had much time to himself. This pleased him. He visited many churches. He said Mass at many altars. He visited many holy shrines where relics were on display. Pilgrims were encouraged and eager to worship these relics. Among them supposedly were bits of Jesus' cross, the chains that held St. Paul as a prisoner, thorns from Jesus' crown, hair from the Virgin Mary, a twig from the burning bush that Moses saw. The number of relics was so great that it was impossible to see them all. The people were told that thousands of years of indulgence could be had by looking at and admiring these objects.

Luther also believed that great spiritual benefits could be gained by adoring the relics and visiting the various holy places. During the four weeks in Rome he tried to accumulate as many blessings as he possible could for himself and his relatives. He even wished that his parents were dead so that he could shorten their years in purgatory by praying for them at the shrines. The most famous relic was Pilate's stairway, which the church said was miraculously brought from Jerusalem to Rome. Anyone who climbed the twenty-eight steps on his hands and knees and said a prayer on each step would receive forgiveness of sins for nine years for each step. Luther crept up the stairs, but as he reached the top of the stairway, he asked himself. "Who knows whether this is true?"

But during the four weeks Luther also saw and heard many things that troubled him. He was shocked to find that many priests were insincere and careless about their work. To him the Mass was a very sacred ceremony. Yet some of the priests spoke the Mass so fast that no one could understand them. Luther asked, "Do all the priests in Rome rush through the Mass like that? It seems meaningless." He was told that many did. Stories about crimes and immoral living among the people, even among some priests and bishops, distressed him greatly. How could this be in holy Rome!

The church officials finally reached a decision about the matter that had been presented to them. Although the answer was not satisfactory, there was nothing more that Luther and his companion could do, so they prepared to return to Germany. They left Rome in January 1511 and reached Augsburg at the beginning of March. Luther had seen, heard, and experienced much during his stay in Rome. Although some things distressed him, his faith in the Catholic Church at that time had not been ruined. But he had been greatly disillusioned. His mind was filled with many troubling questions.

VI

THE PROFESSOR AND PREACHER

After a short stay in Erfurt, Luther was transferred back to the University of Wittenberg to teach theology. Although Wittenberg was an insignificant town of only two-thousand people, Luther was pleased to go to Wittenberg. There he would have the opportunity to intensify his study of God's Word. Wittenberg would be his home for the rest of his life. But, more important, in Wittenberg he would learn to know the true and only way to salvation. Through the study of God's Word he would learn that salvation has been obtained for all people through the atoning work of Jesus Christ. All who believe in Christ as their Redeemer are saved. Eventually this wonderful message of salvation would be proclaimed throughout the world.

An Important Decision

Luther was assigned a little room in the upper story of the Black Cloister. This tower room would be his work room for the most of his life. Here, through the study of God's Word and the guidance of the Holy Spirit, he would find peace for his soul and for untold numbers of others. Thanks to Luther's work, many would again be able to hear the gospel of salvation in all its truth and purity. "God moves in mysterious ways his wonders to perform."

One day Luther was visiting with his good friend Dr. John Staupitz in the garden of the Black Cloister. During the conversation Dr. Staupitz said to Luther, "Brother Martin, you must become a doctor of theology and a preacher. That will give you plenty to do." Staupitz had learned to know Luther as a gifted and dedicated man who had leadership ability. He had in mind that Luther should become the head professor in the religion department at the University and also serve as preacher in the university chapel. This was a great honor, but the work and responsibilities that John Staupitz wanted him to assume frightened Luther. Martin gave Staupitz many reasons why he felt that he could not carry out the assignment, but his friend would not consider any of them as valid reasons. Finally Luther said, "All this work and these responsibilities will kill me. I will be dead in less than three months." Staupitz replied, "God will surprise you. He will be there to help you. Would it be so bad to die in a service that will give life to others?" Jokingly he added, "And, the Lord has need for capable people also in heaven."

Luther finally agreed to pursue his studies in religion and to prepare himself for the position as head professor of religion and as preacher in the university chapel. He studied diligently. In October 1512 he received his doctor's degree in theology. When the degree was conferred on him, he had to swear to preach the Word of God faithfully. This troubled him very much. Later in life he said, "I was made a doctor of theology, but I did not yet know the light."

Light in God's Word

Martin Luther took his vow very seriously. As professor and preacher he had to expound the Scriptures to the students. This required careful and thorough preparation. From 1513 to 1517 he lectured on Genesis, the Psalms,

Romans, and Galatians. Gradually, as he studied the Bible in its original languages, Luther learned to know Christ as St. Paul knew him. But it was not easy for Luther to discard the beliefs and fear that had been implanted in his mind up till now by his parents, his teachers, and the church. But the more he studied the Bible the more he realized that it is God who declares a person righteous through the righteousness earned by his Son. Jesus Christ kept the Law that man could not keep, and he gave his life to pay the punishment for the sins of all. In Paul's Epistle to the Romans he read: "For I am not ashamed of the gospel of Christ: for it is the power of God unto salvation to everyone that believeth; to the Jew first, and also to the Greek. For therein is the righteousness of God revealed from faith to faith: as is written, the just shall live by faith." This passage now took on an altogether new meaning. Man does not become righteous by doing good works. Instead, salvation is a free gift of God through faith in Christ. Man is justified not by works, but by faith alone!

The more he searched the Scriptures, the more Luther's doubts and fears left him, and peace came to his soul. And that saving message of the gospel he had found in the Bible he also proclaimed in his lectures and sermons. It could not be otherwise. Students flocked to his classroom to hear God's Word expounded as they had never heard it explained in the past. They especially appreciated the thoroughness with which Dr. Luther prepared his lectures and the straightforwardness with which he spoke to them. There was never any doubt about his views on a subject. The faculty members of the university were also impressed by Luther's understanding and clear interpretation of the Scriptures.

Luther was a very busy man. In addition to lecturing and preaching at the university, he also was overseer of ten Augustinian monasteries. When the pastor of the City Church in Wittenberg became ill, Martin Luther was assigned to serve as pastor of that large congregation. This increased his work load very much. Luther was an eloquent preacher, but more importantly he had a wonderful message for the people — the gospel of salvation through faith in Christ. More and more people came to hear him. Often he had to preach every day of the week, and sometimes twice a day. Although Luther was teaching and preaching that man is justified by faith in the atonement of Christ, and not by works, he still consided himself a faithful member of the church. He was even convinced that the pope would agree with him.

The Evil of Indulgences

As the pastor of a congregation, Luther was responsible for the spiritual welfare of its members. He felt that some things were practiced and permitted in the church that were wrong and harmful to the people. One such matter was the misuse of indulgences. Originally an indulgence was a letter or certificate issued by the church that released a person from earthly punishment for certain sins that he had committed. For example, an indulgence might release a person from an obligation to make a pilgrimage to a holy place, such as Rome or Jerusalem, or from an obligation to fast for a certain number of days. If it was impossible for a person to make the pilgrimage, he could obtain an indulgence by giving the church a specified amount of money. In time, however, the common people came to believe that indulgences freed them from their sins. They thought that they were buying the forgiveness of sins when they bought an indulgence, and the church made no effort to correct this false belief. After a while, the people were told that they could even buy indulgences that shortened the time of suffering in purgatory for relatives and friends who had died. The church even permitted people to believe that some expensive indulgences freed them from punishment for sins they were planning to commit. The people were told that indulgences were valid because they drew on the surplus of good works that the saints had accumulated. The sale of indulgences became a very profitable business venture for the church. The income from indulgences helped in the establishment and maintenance of churches, cathedrals, and universities.

At the time, the pope was in need of much money to rebuild St. Peter's Church in Rome. In order to increase the sale of indulgences, he granted certain churches and individuals the right to sell indulgences throughout Europe. The Castle Church in Wittenberg was also granted that right. Over the years Elector Frederick of Saxony had gathered and obtained more than nineteen-thousand so-called holy relics, which he put on display at certain times in his Castle Church. The relics supposedly included the teeth of several saints, a piece of cloth from Mary's veil, a piece of cloth in which the Christ-child was wrapped, and a gold piece brought by the Wise Men. The people were told that if they viewed the relics and made a certain contribution, they would receive an indulgence that would reduce their time of suffering in purgatory. And added contributions would reduce the time of suffering for their loved ones.

As pastor of the City Church, Luther felt that it was his duty to tell the people that the forgiveness of sins could not be obtained from God by adoring relics and making contributions to the church, but that salvation is a gift of God through the atonement of Christ. In 1516 he preached three times against the misuse of indulgences. This did not please Elector Frederick of Saxony because part of the income from the sale of indulgences was intended to help support his Castle Church and the University of Wittenberg which he had established.

In 1515 the pope granted Bishop Albert of Brandenburg the right to promote a special sale of indulgences in Germany. Albert appointed a priest by the name of John Tetzel to be his salesman. Tetzel went from town to town carrying a large red cross with the pope's coat of arms. He would set up for business in the town squares. First he would preach a sermon telling the pople about the terrible torments that awaited them if they did not receive remission of their sins. Then he would tell them that remission of sins could be obtained right then and there by purchasing an indulgence. He said, "I have here indulgences for everyone. There is no sin so great that an indulgence cannot remit. No repentance is necessary. I have indulgences for both the living and the dead. I have saved more people from the torments of purgatory than St. Peter by his sermons.

As soon as the money in the coffer rings,
The soul out of purgatory springs."

Many people bought indulgences from him and went away thinking that their money had obtained forgiveness of sins before God.

When John Tetzel came to Saxony in 1517 to offer his indulgences in Wittenberg and other cities, Elector Frederick would not permit it. He was afraid that Tetzel's sales would hurt his own indulgence sales in the Castle Church. But Tetzel was not stopped from making his indulgences available to the people in Wittenberg. He set up his business in the town of Jueterbock, about 25 miles away. Many members of Luther's congregation went to Jueterbock to buy Tetzel's indulgences. When Luther became aware of what his parishioners were doing, he became greatly alarmed. Tetzel was misleading them. Luther told his people, "It is an error to teach and believe that papal indulgences free you from your sins. The forgiveness of sins cannot be bought with money."

The Concerned Pastor and Professor Takes Action

Martin Luther was convinced that some action must be taken against the misuse of indulgences. He felt that the time had come to have a thorough discussion about the doctrine of the forgiveness of sins. In a few days the Feast of All Saints Day would be celebrated in the Castle Church. Parishioners, professors, students, and pilgrims would be coming to the church to worship and buy indulgences. Any

41

announcement posted on the door of the church would be read by many people. So Luther decided to use the church door for an important announcement and for stating his views about indulgences.

Luther carefully prepared his list of ninety-five theses, or paragraphs, in the tower room of the Black Cloister. The theses were not directed against the teachings of the Catholic Church, or even against indulgences themselves, but only against the misuse of indulgences as practiced by John Tetzel and others. Luther wrote: "In the desire for clarifying the truth a disputation (debate) will be held on the following propositions at Wittenberg under the presidency of the Rev. Martin Luther, Augustinian Monk." Then followed the ninety-five paragraphs in which he clearly stated his opinions about sin and forgiveness. We quote from three of the theses:

> When our Lord and Master Jesus Christ says, "Repent," he desires that the whole life of the believer would be one of repentance.

> When true repentance is awakened in a man, full forgiveness from punishment and sin comes to him without any letters of indulgence.

> All believers in the Savior automatically share in the merits earned by Jesus Christ and receive them without the purchase of letters of indulgence.

On October 31, 1517 Luther walked to the Castle Church and nailed the *Ninety-five Theses* to the door. Then he returned to the Black Cloister. He hoped that what he did would lead to a debate with learned theologians. That, he hoped, would help clarify the matter about the forgiveness of sins and the sale of indulgences. He did not know that the posting of his theses would mark the beginning of the reformation of the church. The thought that he was attacking the Roman Catholic Church never entered his mind. Later he said, "I was then a monk and a papist and would readily have murdered any person who denied obedience to

"When our Lord and Master Jesus Christ says, 'Repent,' he desires that the whole life of the believer would be one of repentance."

the pope." He thought that the pope was not aware of the abuses in the sale of indulgences and that he did not know about the harm that Tetzel was doing to the church in Germany.

The next day, November 1, was the All Saint's Day Festival. Crowds of people came to Wittenberg to celebrate. Many came to view the relics and to obtain indulgences in the Castle Church. They saw the placard that Luther had posted on the church door. Students and priests read the Latin theses and discussed them. When the common people saw the lively discussions, they asked the students to translate the theses into German — which they gladly did. They did more. They copied them and gave them to the printers. Within weeks, almost all of Germany knew about Luther's theses. Students, priests, professors, and lay people were all talking about them, but no one accepted the invitation to debate them with Luther. Within a few months copies were available in England, Spain, and Hungary. Many agreed with Luther. "God willing, that man will do something," they said. "He will restore the truth."

Tetzel and others condemned Luther and called him a false prophet and a heretic. The Bishop of Brandenburg accused Luther of attacking the church. He wrote to Luther, "You must realize that by your actions you are being disloyal to the pope and to the emperor."

VII

THE
REFORMER

During the months that followed the posting of the theses, Luther quietly continued to do his work as teacher and pastor. He knew that his theses were being read and discussed throughout Europe, but little did he realize that soon he would have to contend and do battle with the most powerful organization on earth — the Roman Catholic Church.

Reaction from the Church Leaders

Luther expected that the church leaders, especially the pope, would support him in his effort to correct the abuses in the sale of indulgences and in other practices of the church. At the time he had posted the theses, he also wrote a letter to Albert, the Archbishop of Mainz. In this letter he pointed out how Tetzel was misleading the people. A copy of the *Ninety-five Theses* was enclosed with the letter. Luther was hopeful that the archbishop would stop Tetzel. He sincerely hoped that the leaders in the church would discuss with him the abuses to which he referred in his theses. But the archbishop was not about to oppose a good source of income for the church and for himself. Instead of encouraging Luther, the archbishop wrote to the pope in Rome. He asked the pope to order Luther to stop speaking and writing against the sale of indulgences.

Leo X had recently become the new pope of the Catholic Church. At first he was not much concerned about Luther and his theses. He regarded the whole matter as a harmless squabble between two German monks. He said, "A drunken German must have written this. He'll change his mind when he becomes sober." He thought that the problem could easily be taken care of by John Staupitz, Luther's superior in the Augustinian Order. He wrote to the general of the Augustinian order and told him to ask Staupitz to speak to the young monk and convince him that the *Ninety-five Theses* were not in agreement with the teachings of the church. That certainly was not what Luther had expected. He said, "I had hoped that the pope would support me. I had so fortified my theses with proofs from the Bible and papal decrees that I was sure he would condemn Tetzel and bless me. But where I expected benediction from Rome, there came thunder and lightning instead, and I was treated like the sheep that had roiled the wolf's water."

In April a general meeting of the Augustinian order was held in Heidelberg, about two-hundred-seventy miles west of Wittenberg. Luther and Staupitz attended the meeting. As it turned out, the main topic of discussion was not the sale of indulgences, but the doctrine of the church pertaining to good works. The Heidelberg professors were friendly and respectful to Luther even though they were not in complete agreement with his teachings. They listened attentively to his presentations and were impressed with his knowledge of the Scriptures and his sound judgments. The conference did not order Luther to discontinue his preaching and teaching. Before this conference adjourned a resolution was passed asking Luther to write a detailed explanation of his theses and to give the pamphlet to John Staupitz. Staupitz, in turn, was to forward it to the pope.

Luther was pleased with the Heidelberg meeting. He had not been told to keep silent, and he sensed that many of his Augustininan brothers were in sympathy with his views.

On May 15, 1518 Luther returned to Wittenberg. The next morning he preached a strong sermon in the Castle Church on the power of excommunication. Some enemies of Luther from the Dominican order were in church and heard Luther say, "Not every person who is excommunicated will be eternally lost." Later they prepared a set of false theses in which they twisted and changed Luther's words and thoughts in order to make him appear to be a most dangerous heretic. These forged theses were spread throughout Germany under Luther's name. A copy was sent to Cardinal Cajetan. On August 5 Cajetan sent the theses together with an imperial letter to the pope. In this letter the emperor asked the Curia, the pope's court, to ban Luther for his heretical teachings. The Curia agreed. Leo X authorized Cajetan to arrest Luther at once and to bring him to Rome to stand trial. The pope also asked the Elector of Saxony and the general of the Augustinians to deliver the "son of perdition" to Cajetan.

The papal summons reached Luther on August 7th. He was to appear in Rome in 60 days. Luther was in grave danger. His friends were greatly concerned about his safety. They and Luther knew what the church had done to Huss and Savanarola. If the church found him guilty of heresy, he would be condemned to death. An Augustinian brother wrote to Luther, "You are right. You speak the truth, but you will not accomplish anything. Go back to your cell and pray God for protection and mercy." Martin Luther was concerned, but did not lose courage. He said, "The more they threaten, the greater becomes my confidence in God. Wife, children, fields, house, money, possessions I have not. My fame and my name are already torn to bits. All that I have left of me is my frail body. If they deprive me of that too, they will shorten my life, but my soul they can not take from me."

The Friendly Elector

A number of capable and learned men had become Luther's staunch supporters. One of them was Philip Melanchthon, who arrived at Wittenberg in August 1518. He was to be an instructor of Greek at the University of Wittenberg. He soon became one of Luther's best friends and aides. Luther also had gained the respect and admiration of the elector of Saxony, Frederick the Wise. When Luther received the summons to come to Rome to be tried, he appealed to his elector for help. Prince Frederick feared that Luther would not receive a fair hearing in Rome. Therefore he requested that Luther be examined in Germany.

Elector Frederick was one of the most influential electors in Germany and had also found favor with the pope by promising his support in the war with the Turks. Saxony was also a good source of income for the church. Furthermore, an election of a new emperor was about to take place, and there was a good possibility that Frederick might be elected. The good will of the elector therefore was most important to the pope at this time. He could ill afford to deny the elector's request to have Luther examined in Germany. So Leo X informed Elector Frederick that arrangements would be made to try Luther in Germany. Here again we see the hand of God steering the course of history.

Elector Frederick requested that Cardinal Cajetan have Luther examined in Augsburg, Germany. This was agreeable to the pope. At first Luther was to be tried by a jury, but Cajetan suggested that he first meet personally with Luther. The pope agreed, but told Cajetan not to debate church doctrine with Luther. He was to accuse Luther of false teaching and then order him to recant. If he refused to recant, Cajetan was to condemn him as a false teacher and heretic, but not to arrest him — not yet.

Luther Meets with Cardinal Cajetan

On September 25, 1518 Luther set out on foot for Augsburg. He traveled with a friend, Brother Leonard Beier.

Although he had a letter of safe conduct, Luther was troubled. He knew what it could mean for him. He said, "I have the stake before my eyes constantly." In Weimar a Franciscan monk warned him, "Dear doctor, the Italians are learned men. I fear that you will not be able to stand your ground against them and that you will be convicted and burned." Luther replied, "Even in Augsburg in the midst of his enemies, Christ reigns."

Luther did not know what to expect in his meeting with Cardinal Cajetan. The first meeting took place on October 13. The cardinal received him in a kind manner. He hoped to persuade Luther and to win him back by assuming a kind and fatherly attitude. Luther was pleased with the reception, but he was eager to discuss the matters that brought about the meeting. He wanted clarification of the misunderstanding that apparently had developed between him and some church leaders.

Cajetan then explained his reason for the meeting, "I have been ordered by the pope to require three things of you. First, you are to repent of your errors and renounce them. Secondly, you are to promise not to teach them in the future. Thirdly, you are to stop all activities that disturb the peace of the church." Luther asked Cajetan to name the errors and to prove that they were errors indeed on the basis of Scripture. Although the cardinal was told by the pope that he should not debate with Luther, he found himself taking part in several heated arguments during the three-day meeting. Again and again during the discussions he shouted, "Recant! Acknowledge that you are wrong. Only this will save you from the pope!" Finally, after he realized that Luther stood firm in his conviction that he had taught nothing contrary to the Bible, Cajetan cried out, "Go! Recant or never come to see me again."

After the last meeting with Luther, Cajetan had a brief meeting with John Staupitz. He asked Staupitz to try to persuade Luther to recant. Staupitz promised nothing but agreed that he would ask Luther to write a letter to the cardinal. This Luther did. In the letter he apologized for losing his temper, but he again stated that his conscience would not permit him to recant.

There were rumors that plans had been made to arrest Luther and take him to Rome. So on the night of October 20 Luther's friends secretly led him out of the city of Augsburg through a small gate. A messenger was waiting there with two horses. Luther was helped into the saddle, and the two rode off toward Wittenberg. On the 31st of October, just a year after posting the *Ninety-five Theses*, Luther arrived in Wittenberg. He was home, but he knew he was not safe. He expected a papal "bull of excommunication" any day. His friend, John Staupitz, advised him to leave Germany and flee to France. But Luther stayed.

Luther Meets with Carl von Miltitz

Cajetan was frustrated and angry. He had failed to convince Luther that his teachings were false. He had failed to get Luther to recant. In November he wrote two letters, one to Pope Leo, the other to Elector Frederick of Saxony. In these letters he described the discussions he had had with Luther in Augsburg. He accused Luther of heresy and told the elector that he was honor-bound to arrest Luther and to send him to Rome. The elector sent a copy of the letter to Luther for comments. Luther pointed out to the elector that Cajetan had neither designated the false teachings of which he was accusing him, nor proved him guilty of heresy. Frederick had no thought of delivering his university professor to Rome without a fair trial. In December he sent a letter to Cardinal Cajetan in which he rejected Cajetan's request to arrest Luther. The elector had taken his stand. This would mean much for Luther in the days and years ahead.

The pope was determined to have Luther delivered to Rome. Elector Frederick was just as determined that, if Luther should be tried at all, he would be tried in Germany. Pope Leo now made his move to overcome that obstacle. He chose his chamberlain, Charles von Miltitz, to persuade the elector to change his mind and persuade Luther to come to Rome to recant. When Miltitz left for Germany, he was confident that he would succeed in his mission. The pope had given him special indulgences for the elector's Castle Church in Wittenberg. In them the pope promised greatly to reduce the years of suffering in purgatory for the Wittenbergers. That should please the elector. Miltitz was also to present Frederick with the "Golden Rose," an honor that the pope bestowed on only a few very select people. Frederick recognized these things as bribes, and he did nothing to indicate that he was changing his mind about Luther.

The pope had ordered Miltitz not to argue with Luther, but to persuade him that it would be to his advantage to come to Rome and to make peace with the pope. Frederick agreed to arrange a meeting between Luther and Miltitz at Altenburg. In the meeting Luther absolutely refused to recant, but two agreements were reached that were satisfactory to all parties: First, Luther would stop all disputes about indulgences if his enemies would stop attacking him. Secondly, Miltitz was to ask the pope to appoint a German bishop to point out the errors in Luther's theses. Luther also agreed to recant any proven errors.

After the conference Miltitz took Luther to dinner. During the meal he told Luther that on his journey he discovered that only two or three out of every five men he had met supported the pope. When the two men parted, Miltitz hugged Luther and gave him a kiss of peace. Later Luther said, "I was very suspicious of his motives, but I promised nothing that would hinder me from preaching and teaching the truths of Scriptures."

The Leipzig Debate

Luther returned to Wittenberg and concentrated on his lectures and his study of God's Word. He published nothing that related to his differences with the church. But his enemies did not keep silent. Before long, Luther found himself in a dispute that marked the parting of the ways between him and his followers and the Catholic Church.

Dr. John Eck, professor at the University of Ingolstadt, broke the silence when he bitterly attacked Luther's *Ninety-five Theses*. Luther replied by writing a series of articles in which he strongly defended himself. Professor Carlstadt of the University of Wittenberg also came to Luther's defense. Eck was very shrewd and was eager to engage Martin Luther in a public debate, but he could hardly challenge a man who had been declared a heretic. He therefore challenged Carlstadt. Carlstadt accepted the challenge and invited Luther to accompany him, which he was glad to do. Here at last Luther saw an opportunity to debate publicly the issues raised in the theses he had posted on October 31, 1517.

The debate took place in a large auditorium at the University of Leipzig. The meeting with Eck consisted of a series of discussions and disputes that lasted more than two weeks, from June 27 to July 15, 1519. Luther, Carlstadt, Amsdorf, and Melanchthon represented the University of Wittenberg.

Carlstadt and Eck argued for a week about free will and grace. Toward the end of the week it became evident that Carlstadt was no match for the shrewd Eck. On July 4 Luther took over for Carlstadt. The subject under discussion was the development of the papacy. Luther argued that the office of the pope was not based on Scripture, but was man-made. He pointed out that the Greek Catholic Church had never recognized the pope in Rome. Many other questions were raised and debated by the two men. They argued about the infallibility of the pope, purgatory, indulgences, penance, the Mass. Luther based his arguments on the Bible. Eck considered the teachings and traditions of the Catholic Church the supreme authority in matters of faith.

At one point in the debate Eck accused Luther of being a follower of Huss, who had been condemned by the church and burned at the stake in 1415. To that Luther replied, "I hold that it is not necessary for salvation to believe that the Roman Catholic Church is superior to others. I do not care whether this comes from Wycliffe or from Huss. . . . It is not in the power of the Roman pope to construct articles of faith. . . . By divine law we are forbidden to believe anything which is not established by divine Scripture." Eck shouted "Luther, I command you to recant your false opinion and to vow faithfulness to the Church which alone has salvation!" When Eck got Luther to make the admission that he believed that church councils and popes can err and have erred, many people believed that the Leipzig debate was a victory for John Eck. In their opinion Eck had proved beyond a doubt that Luther was a false teacher and a heretic.

The debate with Eck was a turning point for Luther. It had clarified many things for him. He realized now that not certain individuals but the Catholic Church as such had placed the authority of man above the authority of God's Word. He also was convinced that the church would not give up its false teachings and that a division was coming. This saddened him greatly.

The following may have been part of a conversation between Melanchthon and Luther as they journeyed back to Wittenberg:

Melanchthon: These meetings with Eck have shaken my faith in the teachings of the church. What are your thoughts, Martin?

Luther: My faith in the church is also shaken. Sinful man has replaced the holy Word of God with his own thoughts and words. God's Word now stands second to man's word in the church.

Melanchthon: Is there any hope that the church can be made to see her errors?

Luther: We have tried. Others have tried. I am afraid it is too late.

Melanchthon: What can be done? Thousands of souls are being misled by the church.

Luther: We can preach; we can teach; we can write; we can publish. We can expose the falsehoods and errors of the church and we'll do so on the basis of God's Word. God's Word will be our weapon. With God and his Word on our side we shall gain the victory over the powers of darkness.

Luther's Call for Reformation

Luther returned to Wittenberg with renewed determination to do all he could to combat the spiritual evils that had plagued the people for so many years. The cell in the Black Cloister was his workshop. There his mind and pen worked tirelessly to produce tracts, pamphlets, and books. In one year alone the printers published 133 of his writings, for which he refused to receive any royalties. It is hard to understand how he could do all that writing in addition to attending to his regular duties as professor and pastor. He said, "God has given me a swift hand and good memory. When I write, it just flows out. I don't have to press and squeeze." His writings were circulated far and wide and were eagerly read. Luther recognized the printing press as a God-given means to bring the truth to thousands who could not be reached by his voice. And it was mainly through his publications that support for his cause continued to grow, not only in Germany but also in many other countries.

In 1520 Luther produced three very important documents that had far-reaching effects. In his *Address to the German Nobility,* Luther urged the princes of Germany to do everything within their power to improve conditions in the church and state. He blamed the church leaders for much that was wrong and evil in the church and state. He pointed out that the authority of the pope should be restricted to spiritual matters. Civil matters are not the responsibility of the church, but of the state. In the church the clergy had also assumed too much power. It had no right to lord it over the people. All believers are equal before God and have the right and duty to read, interpret, and proclaim the Word of God. Luther also suggested definite steps that should be taken to correct the disorder and evils that existed in the church and the state.

In *The Babylonian Captivity of the Church,* Luther attacked the teaching that the seven sacraments of the church were the only means by which anyone could gain God's saving grace. First of all, he pointed out, a sacrament must be instituted by God. Christ established only two sacraments, Baptism and the Lord's Supper, not seven. Furthermore, the power and benefits of the sacraments do not come from the priest who administers them, but from the Word of God in the sacrament. The power of forgiveness comes from the word of promise in the sacrament. But only those who believe the word of promise receive its benefits. Without faith in the promise there is no forgiveness. Justification is by faith alone. In discussing the Lord's Supper, Luther stated that the church was in error when it taught that the priest transformed bread and wine into the body and blood of Christ and that he sacrificed Christ over and over again for the sins of the people. He said that not only the priest, but everyone should receive both the bread and wine in the Lord's Supper. Christ said to *all* who were present when he instituted the sacrament, "Take eat. Take drink."

The Freedom of a Christian Man was the shortest of the three documents Luther wrote in 1520. Luther began by saying, "A Christian man is a perfectly free lord, subject to none. A Christian man is a perfectly dutiful servant, subject to all." That sounds like a contradiction. What Luther meant was that since a Christian is saved through faith in Christ Jesus, he is free from guilt and fear. And since the Christian now belongs to Christ, he will want to show his appreciation for his salvation by deeds of kindness and love. Not the fear of God's wrath and punishment, as the church taught, should cause man to do good works; but truly good works flow only out of faith in Christ.

These three treatises were Luther's call for reformation. Their impact was great throughout Europe especially in Rome. Many who did not agree with Luther accused him of dividing the church and of trying to found a new church. But he was not trying to establish a new church. Luther hoped to restore the authority of the Word of God in the church and to expose the falsehoods that had hidden the gospel for so many years.

VIII

THE ACCUSED

Luther knew that he had spoken the truth, but he knew that Rome very likely would condemn him and do everything possible to destroy him. A showdown had to come between him and the pope and between him and the emperor. The church was the first to act.

The Papal Bull

In November 1519 the Curia met in Rome to discuss the steps that should be taken to stop Luther. Eck urged that the pope should act immediately to silence once and for all "that beast of Wittenberg," as he called Luther. The Curia decided, however, to make another attempt to get the Elector Frederick to surrender Luther to Rome. Frederick replied that arrangements had already been made for a meeting between Luther and Miltitz. At that meeting the archbishop of Trier was to serve as judge. The meeting with the archbishop, however, did not take place; but that, he said, was through no fault of his own. Frederick also made it quite clear that he had no intention of surrendering Luther to Rome. He was determined that his famous university professor should have a fair trial, and he knew that he would not get that in Rome. So the elector informed Luther that it was his plan to take him along to the diet at Worms, where his case could be heard.

In March 1520 the pope appointed a commission of four with Eck as chairman. This commission was ordered to draw up a bull of excommunication against Luther. On June 1st the bull, or papal pronouncement, was unanimously accepted by the cardinals. On June 15, 1520 the pope signed the bull and affixed the papal seal. It was ready for printing and for distribution throughout the church.

The bull was a lengthy document that listed and condemned forty-one of Luther's writings. In it the pope lamented that anything so wicked could have taken place among the Germans for whom he always had a special affection. He called God to witness that he had done everything possible to bring Luther back to the fold of the church. The bull stated that Luther's attacks on the papacy and his false teaching dare not be tolerated. It then condemned Luther as a heretic and stated that he would be excommunicated unless he recanted within sixty days. Excommunication meant that he could not partake of the sacraments of the church, his property would be taken away from him and all his writings would be burned. After his excommunication he would be in great danger of being put under the ban of the state, cruelly punished, and possibly put to death.

In July the pope ordered John Eck and Jerome Aleander to publish and display the bull in Germany. Eck was to distribute it throughout Saxony, Luther's state, but he found it very difficult to carry out his assignment. He found that Luther's writings were being read by thousands. Many of them believed that God had at last sent them a deliverer from the tyranny of the papacy. These people were not about to join in the condemnation of a man who had not even been granted a fair trial. When Eck tried to post and distribute the document in Leipzig, the university students almost caused a riot. He had to find safety in the Dominican monastery. Aleander didn't fare much better. When he built a fire in Louvain to burn Luther's writings, the students began throwing official Catholic writings into his fire. When the archbishop finally forbade the burning of Luther's books, the citizens walked around the city chanting slogans that supported Luther.

Luther's Reaction to the Bull

The papal bull did not reach Luther until October. He immediately wrote a sharp reply which he called "Against the Evil Bull of the Antichrist." He wrote in part: "I protest before God, our Lord Jesus, his sacred angels, and the whole world that with my whole heart I dissent from the damnation of this bull, that I curse it as a sacrilege. If the pope does not retract and condemn the bull and punish Dr. Eck, then no one is to doubt that he is God's enemy, Christ's persecutor, Christendom's destroyer, and the true Antichrist. Christ will judge whose excommunication will stand."

On December 10 the sixty days were up, but Luther had no thought of recanting. In fact, he had spent very little time discussing the bull and his excommunication with anyone. He kept on with his lectures at the university. His classes had always been well attended, but now even more students flocked to his classroom to hear him.

Luther's excommunication was now officially in effect. He was out of the Catholic Church, and all his writings were to be burned. But Luther and Melanchthon had a different book-burning in mind. Early on the morning of December 10 Melanchthon posted this notice on the Castle Church and university bulletin boards: "The spiteful books of the papal theology will be given to the flames, even as the enemies of the gospel have burned the scriptural writings of Luther. All interested in this event meet at the east gate of the city." By nine o'clock a large number of townspeople and students had gathered outside the Elster Gate to see what would happen. A wood fire was started by some stu-

"Because you angered the Holy One of God, let the Lord consume you in these flames."

dents. Then from the University came a procession of students and professors led by Martin Luther. As the flames leaped up, the students and professors threw Roman Cath- olic books and pamphlets and copies of the canon law into the fire. Suddenly Luther stepped forward with the papal bull in his hand. He held it up for everyone to see, and then as he threw it into the flames he said, "Because you angered the Holy One of God, let the Lord consume you in these flames!" In this dramatic way Martin Luther broke forever his ties with the Roman Catholic Church. Later he said, "I, Martin Luther, make known hereby to everyone that by my wish, advice, and act the books of the pope of Rome were burned."

After the gathering had sung the Te Deum ("We Praise Thee, O God"), the professors left, but the students were not yet ready to return to the university. For some time they stood around the fire singing funeral songs in honor of the burnt papal bull. Then they marched through the streets of Wittenberg shouting and singing.

The Summons from the Emperor

Luther had dared to defy the pope. What would happen now? On January 3, 1521 Pope Leo X announced the formal excommunication of Martin Luther and his followers. The pope thereby decreed that everyone was to consider Luther and his supporters heretics and heathen. The church had excommunicated Luther, but that was where its power ended. It could not imprison him or punish him by death. That power belonged to the state, but Luther knew he was not safe. His enemies were still scheming to take him to Rome or to kill him. He told his students that he expected to die a martyr's death. Luther and the elector of Saxony had appealed to the emperor for a hearing at the diet, or assembly, which was in session in Worms at that time. Charles V, a young man only twenty years old, was the new emperor. He was a loyal Catholic who had sworn allegiance to the pope, but he knew that Luther had many followers in Germany and that Elector Frederick was a very influential and strong-willed man. He therefore agreed to permit Luther to appear at the diet for a hearing. On March 26 the emperor's messengers delivered this summons to Luther at Wittenberg: "Dear esteemed and honorable Dr. Luther: We and the states of the holy empire here assembled, having resolved to institute an inquiry touching the doctrines and books that you have lately published, have issued for your coming and return to a place of safety our safe conduct.

"Our sincere desire is that you should prepare immediately for this journey in order that within a space of twenty-one days fixed by safe conduct you may without fail present yourself before the diet. Fear neither injustice or violence." The summons was signed, "Charles V, Emperor."

Although Luther expected to be summoned to Worms, he was taken aback when the royal messenger himself appeared at the door of the Black Cloister with the summons. He, of course, would go, but many thoughts came to his mind. Within a few days he would be standing before none other than Emperor Charles V and the highest tribunal of the empire. His life would be in their hands. Would he be permitted to speak and defend himself? What would their verdict be? He had been promised safe conduct to and from Wittenberg. But would he really be safe? Huss had also been promised safe conduct, but he never returned to his home. He was burned at the stake. The one thought that occupied his mind more than any other was that now God was giving him a wonderful opportunity to witness to the truth. He looked forward to the meeting, even though he knew that his life was in grave danger. He said, "This is the Lord's cause. I commend myself to him. He who saved the three men in the fiery furnace will also preserve me."

On to Worms

On March 26, 1521 the imperial herald, Kasper Sturm, arrived to escort Luther to Worms. The journey began on April 2. Luther rode in a wagon accompanied by the herald and three friends, Professor Amsdorf, an Augustinian monk, and a student. A three-hundred-mile journey lay ahead, but it turned out to be more of a triumphal procession than a journey. In every town and city people turned out to cheer and encourage Luther. They wanted to see the brave man who was so daring as to set himself against pope and emperor. Some feared for his life. They said, "Since there are so many cardinals and bishops at the diet, he will doubtless be burned to a powder in short order as was Huss at Constance." To this Luther replied, "Even if they kindled a fire as high as heaven from Wittenberg to Worms, I will appear in the name of the Lord, in obedience to the summons, and confess Christ." On the way they passed through Leipzig, Erfurt, Frankfurt, and Naumburg. The mayor of Naumburg honored Luther by inviting him to dinner. Outside Erfurt the university student body met him and accompanied him to his quarters in the Augustinian monastery. On April 7 he preached by special request in the Augustinian church, which was crowded to overflowing. While in Frankfurt Luther received a letter from his friend Spalatin. He wrote that Elector Frederick had asked him to advise Luther not to continue on to Worms because he could no longer protect him. He had heard that Luther would most likely be condemned and put under the imperial ban. But Luther did not permit himself to be frightened. He said, "Even if there are as many devils in Worms as there are tiles on the roofs, I will enter the city."

On the morning of April 16 Luther's wagon was nearing Worms. Sturm, the imperial herald, rode ahead of the wagon. Suddenly a large number of horsemen came riding out from the city. They had been sent to escort Luther into Worms. A crowd of several thousand cheered and called Luther's name as the procession moved down the street. Somewhat embarrassed, Luther waved to the people and said, "God bless you." The wagon stopped at the House of the Knights of St. John, where the elector had arranged lodging for Luther and his friends.

Luther Before the Diet

Both Luther and Elector Frederick had requested that the hearing take place before a committee appointed by the diet. At first the diet agreed to this, but on April 17 Luther was told that he was to make his appearance before the diet itself. He was also told to conduct himself courteously and not to speak except when answering questions. At four o'clock, Pappenheim, the imperial marshal and Sturm, the herald, conducted Luther to the episcopal palace. The streets were crowded with people so that they had to use side streets and alleys to get to the palace. After waiting two hours, Pappenheim and Sturm led Luther into the court chamber. He was accompanied by his friend and legal advisor, Jerome Schurf.

There Luther stood facing the most distinguished and powerful officials of the state and church. He was only thirty-seven years old, but he had experienced much. He was well informed and had successfully debated with some of the most capable men of his time. But, above all, he knew that God and his holy Word were his sure defense. The emperor Charles V, sat on a throne surrounded by the electoral princes, archbishops, ministers, and secretaries. Charles whispered to someone near him, "That monk will never make a heretic of me." On a table was a pile of twenty books that Aleander had gathered.

The hearing began. Dr. John Eck (not the same John Eck with whom Luther had debated at Leipzig) began by speaking in a loud voice: "His imperial Majesty has summoned you, Martin Luther, to find out two things: First, are you willing to confess that these books which have been circulated in your name are yours?" Luther was about to answer the question with a "yes," when his counselor, Jerome Schurf, shouted, "Let the titles be read." After the notary had read the titles, Luther declared that the books were his. The second question was, "Are you ready to renounce these books or part of them?" Then Luther requested the diet to grant him time for reflection before answering. He said, "It would be unwise not to reflect and deliberate over the answer to that question, since it involves faith, the salvation of souls, and the Word of God."

After the members of the diet had consulted among themselves, they grudgingly granted Luther twenty-four hours' time to reply to the second question. He was then escorted back to his quarters. There he talked with his friends, read the Scripture, and spent much of the night in prayer. Harmony in the state and church was of prime importance to the emperor and the pope. Not to Luther! To him they were secondary. Truth was most important to him. He had been told that he could not read his answer, but during the night he carefully prepared a draft of what he wanted to say. The next morning he was prepared to give his answer to the second question.

On April 18 shortly before four o'clock Sturm again escorted Luther to the council chambers in the episcopal palace. Arrangements had to be made to use a larger hall since many more people had come to hear Luther's reply. Even the large hall was soon overcrowded. Many had to stand. Dr. Eck opened the meeting with a short speech. Then he repeated the second question he had asked Luther on the previous day: "Are you ready to renounce these books or part of them?" Martin Luther was ready with his answer. He spoke condfidently and without fear, first in Latin, then in German: "Most serene emperor, illustrious princes and lords, I appear before you today to reply to the questions addressed to me yesterday. I apologize if I have not given everyone here present his proper title. If I am guilty of this, I beg your forgiveness since I was not brought up in a prince's palace but in the confines of a monastery. Yesterday two questions were addressed to me. The first I answered when I stated that I am the writer of the books here on this table. I stand by my reply of yesterday. The books are mine. As for the second question, a simple answer will not suffice since I have written on many subjects. There are three classes of

on this table. There are writings in which I speak of ...nd good works. They are so pure and scriptural that ...my enemies agree that they are worthy to be read by all Christians. These books I cannot retract. Another group of books deal with the evils in the church, especially the evils of the papacy under which the German people had to suffer. These I cannot retract because by doing so I would be encouraging the pope to continue misleading the Christian church. The third group of writings consist of books in which I have attacked certain people who defended the errors of the pope and the church. In some instances I used rather harsh language. I apologize for the strong language, but I cannot retract the content of these books. If I am shown that I am in error, I will be the first one to throw all these books into the fire. But, I must warn you to be careful lest by quenching this controversy and dissension you should persecute the holy Word of God and draw down upon yourselves a flood of unbearable evils. I herewith commend myself to your Majesty with the humble plea that you will not permit my accusers to make me hateful in your eyes without cause."

The hearing was not going as Luther's enemies had expected. They wanted only a "yes" or "no" answer to the two questions they had addressed to him. But Luther had taken the opportunity to confess his faith and his conviction that God's Word is the only sure guide in matters pertaining to man's eternal salvation. After some abusive remarks about Luther's address, Dr. Eck said to Luther, "You have not spoken to the point. Give us an answer without elaborations. Do you or do you not retract what you have written in these books?" Luther gave his answer in a clear, firm voice, "Since your majesty demands a simple answer, I will give you one. Unless I am convicted by Scriptures and clear reasoning — I do not trust in popes and councils since they have often been wrong — my conscience is bound to the Word of God. I neither can nor will recant anything, for to act against my conscience is wrong and

"I neither can nor will recant anything, for to act against my conscience is wrong
and dangerous. Here I stand. I cannot do otherwise. God help me. Amen."

dangerous. Here I stand. I cannot do otherwise. God help me. Amen."

There was a short, stunned silence. Then tumult broke out. Eck tried to speak, but he could not be heard above the noise. The emperor signaled to the imperial herald to take Luther away, and then he angrily left the hall. The hearing was over. Friends quickly surrounded Luther and made a way for him out of the hall. As they approached the doorway, the Spaniards shouted, "To the stake! To the stake!" Once outside, Luther raised his arms in triumph and shouted, "I am through! I am through." God had given him the faith and courage to stand firm in his convictions before his most powerful enemies.

The Edict of Worms

Charles V was angry. The next day he summoned the electors and princes to ask their advice. He had already made up his mind to put Luther under the imperial ban. He said, "I wish to proceed against him as a notorious heretic, and ask you to declare yourselves as you promised me." But the electors thought it wise not to condemn Luther without making another effort to persuade him to recant. They knew that Luther had many followers who would come to his defense. Some were powerful German princes. The emperor finally was persuaded to appoint a small committee to confer with Luther. In the discussions with that committee Luther made it very clear that he would recant only if he was proven wrong on the basis of the Bible and clear reason. That the committee would not accept.

The useless meetings dragged on for almost a week. Finally Luther begged Elector Frederick to ask the emperor to grant him permission to return to Wittenberg. The request was granted with the assurance of another safe conduct of twenty-one days. That evening he wrote a letter to the emperor and electors. In it he thanked them for granting him the hearing. He expressed his disappointment that the meetings with the special committee had been fruitless.

He wrote that he wanted nothing more than a reform of the church on the basis of the Bible. He was willing to suffer shame and death for the emperor, but he reserved for himself the liberty to confess and proclaim the Word of God.

On the morning of April 26, Martin Luther left Worms. His friends accompanied him in two wagons. The imperial herald Kaspar Sturm rode ahead. Luther had been given a safe conduct, but he knew that his enemies would stop at nothing to prevent him from reaching Wittenberg. There was a possibility that they might seize him and force him to return as their captive.

Several drafts of the edict against Luther had to be written before a copy was produced that was acceptable to the electors and Charles V. On May 26 the emperor signed the edict (public notice, or decree) outlawing Martin Luther. The edict decreed that no one should have any dealings with Luther. All his books should be burned, and everybody was forbidden to publish or read them. Luther was declared an outlaw of the state, and no one dare give him protection or shelter. It was the duty of any citizen to seize him and deliver him to the emperor. Anyone disobeying the edict would be arrested, punished, and his property taken from him. Would the emperor be able to enforce the edict?

THE KNIGHT

IX

When Elector Frederick saw that things were not going well at the diet, he feared for Luther's safety. He knew that his enemies would try to seize him and kill him as soon as the safe conduct was no longer in effect. He told one of his trusted knights to see to it that Luther would be taken to a safe hiding place. He said, "I want you to arrange to hide Luther somewhere in Saxony, but don't tell me where he is. I don't want to be able to answer any questions regarding his whereabouts." Luther and Amsdorf knew something of what would happen on the way to Wittenberg, but they were not told the details.

Safe at the Wartburg

The two wagons carrying Luther and his friends continued without incident toward Wittenberg. After several days they reached Saxony. Now they all felt more secure. Luther sent the imperial herald Sturm back to Worms. Near Eisenach Luther was secretly told to turn off on a less-traveled road which led to the town of Moehra. Amsdorf and the Augustinian monk were in the same wagon with

Luther. The other wagon continued on the main road to Wittenberg. That evening Luther and his two friends reached Moehra where Luther's uncle, Heinz Luther, lived. They spent the night there. The next afternoon they continued on their journey. Three people were on the wagon with Luther — Amsdorf, the monk Petzensteiner, and the driver of the horses.

Toward evening they were traveling on a narrow road through the dense Thuringian Forest. Suddenly ahead of them they heard the sound of galloping horses. Four or five horsemen rushed out from among the trees. One stopped the wagon by grasping the reins. Another knocked the driver from the wagon. The monk jumped from the wagon and ran into the woods. "Which one is Luther?" one of the horsemen shouted. "I am Luther," Martin answered. The man roughly pulled Luther off the wagon.

Amsdorf put on a good act. "Don't hurt him," he shouted. "Let him go. He's not a criminal. Let him go, you ruffians!" But it did no good. Luther was thrown on a horse. Then they turned their horses and rode off into the forest pulling Luther's horse after them. For several hours they rode in different directions in order to cover their tracks and lose any possible pursuers. Luther knew that he was being taken to a place of safety, but he did not know where. Suddenly ahead of him loomed a high hill with a large castle. It was the Wartburg. This old castle near Eisenach had been chosen as Luther's place of refuge.

Luther and one of his abductors rode up toward the castle. The other horseman galloped down the road and disappeared in the darkness. It was almost midnight when Luther and his escort crossed over the drawbridge into the court of the castle. Luther was warmly greeted by the warden and immediately shown to his quarters.

"Welcome to the Wartburg," said the warden. "I am Hans Berlepsch. These two rooms are your quarters. For the present you must not let yourself be seen by anyone except me and the two pages who will serve you your meals."

"Am I a prisoner here in this castle?" asked Luther.

"No, you are a guest of Elector Frederick, but your stay here must be kept a secret. You are ordered to let your beard and hair grow and to put on the clothes of a knight. From now on you are to be known by everyone as Knight George. In about two weeks, when your hair and beard should hide your identity, you will be able to leave the castle for short periods of time. But someone is always to go with you."

"How long am I to remain here?"

"That I don't know. The elector will determine when it is safe for you to return to Wittenberg."

When the warden had left, Martin looked about his quarters. The rooms were simply furnished with a table, desk, stool, chair, bed, and wash basin. At the end of the larger room was a window. He was exhausted, but before he retired for the night, he knelt down and prayed, "Heavenly Father, thank you for sustaining me during my trial at Worms and for bringing me safely to this place of refuge. Grant that the evil designs and work of my enemies and of the enemies of your Word come to naught. Bless your Word so that many people will find the true way of salvation as it is stated in your holy gospel. Hear my prayer for the sake of him who reconciled us to God, your Son, our Savior. Amen."

It was daylight when Luther awoke. He opened the window in the other room. There before and below him stretched miles and miles of forests, hills, and meadows. Just below the hill nestled the little city of Eisenach, where Luther had received his high school education. The sight from the window was beautiful and peaceful. Birds were flying about and singing. "This is the Land of the Birds," he exclaimed, "but it is also my Patmos." He was thinking of the island to which the Apostle John had been banished by the enemies of the gospel.

Luther appreciated the elector's kindness in making these elaborate arrangements in order to save his life. But he dreaded the isolation to which he would be subjected, possibly for many months. He had been in the forefront of the battle contending for the truth of God's Word, and that is where he preferred to be. It was his fervent prayer that his co-workers, Melanchthon and others, would continuously carry forward the work of the reformation during his enforced absence.

For nearly a year Luther remained hidden in the Wartburg. Only a few close friends knew what had happened to him. Others could only guess where he was. Rumors spread that he had been killed, or that he had been imprisoned, or that he had escaped to another country. Albrecht Duerer, a great artist and admirer of Luther, wrote in his diary, "O God, is Luther dead? Who will now teach us the holy gospel?"

Soon letters arrived in Wittenberg from Luther's hideout with the return address, "The Land of the Birds." When Melanchthon heard that his friend and co-worker was alive and safe, he exclaimed happily," Our beloved father lives. Let us take courage and be firm." Spalatin informed Luther by secret messenger that the emperor had put him under the ban and that he was now to be treated as an outlaw of the state. This greatly disturbed Luther. He had been condemned because he opposed the false and corrupt teachings of the Catholic Church and defended the truths of God's Word.

The Writer and Translator

Martin Luther was not a man who could remain idle. There was work to be done. He couldn't preach, but he could write. And it was here, in the "Land of the Birds," that he did some of his most important writing. At first he had only his Hebrew and Greek Testaments, which he managed to put in his knapsack just before he was kidnapped near Eisenach. At various times Melanchthon and Spalatin secretly provided him with some of the books that he requested.

The amount of writing he did is amazing. In his little room in the Wartburg he wrote many letters, books, and articles. They were sent to Spalatin, who had them printed. One article was titled "Concerning Confession." In this article Luther pointed out that the Roman Catholic Church was wrong when it demanded private confessions from all people. Confession, Luther believed, was a personal matter between the Christian and his God. He should feel free to confess his sins to God whenever he wanted to do so. Another treatise was on monastic vows. He also translated Psalms and wrote sermons that he could preach after he would be released. His greatest accomplishment while at the Wartburg was his translation of the entire New Testament from Greek into German. His one great desire was to produce the Bible in a language that the common people in Germany could read and understand. This was not easy, because Germany did not have one, but many German languages, or dialects. In translating the Bible he had to find German words and expressions that most of the common people could understand. As a result, Luther's German eventually became the unifying language of the German people. When Luther returned to Wittenberg, he kept on reviewing and refining his translation. In the fall of 1522 Luther's German New Testament appeared in print. Copies were bought and eagerly read throughout Germany. More than five-thousand copies were sold in two weeks. The printing presses could not keep up with the demand.

Luther found it hard to leave his books and his writings, but he knew he needed some recreation. He was suffering from insomnia and stomach trouble. The warden urged him to leave his work and to make himself known in the area as Knight George. After his beard and hair were long enough to conceal his identity, he occasionally roamed the woods which he enjoyed. Sometimes he was asked to join a hunting party. He didn't mind the riding, but he found no satisfaction in chasing and killing helpless animals. Once when a little rabbit was cornered, Luther caught it, quickly covered it with his jacket, and hid it in some thick shrubbery, but the dogs found it and killed it. He said, "O pope, and you

too, Satan, just as this helpless rabbit was killed, so you want to destroy souls of men that have been saved by Jesus Christ." Most of all Luther enjoyed walking though the countryside, visiting with the peasant neighbors. They learned to know him as the kind knight who understood their problems and sympathized with them.

Troubles in Wittenberg

Almost ten months had gone by since Luther entered the Wartburg. Except for a brief, unannounced visit to Wittenberg in December, he had not been able to guide the developments there. But soon his knighthood days would be over, and he would enter another important period of his busy life. Martin Luther had hoped that his co-workers in Wittenberg would faithfully carry on the work of the reformation during his absence. But all was not well in Wittenberg.

For some of the leaders in Wittenberg things were progressing too slowly. They wanted to eliminate, or at least change, almost everything that had been customary in the Catholic Church. One of those leaders was Dr. Carlstadt, a professor at the Wittenberg University. Many of the changes he wanted to make were very extreme, even radical. He insisted that all monks, nuns, and priests should marry and that all cloisters and monasteries should be closed. He told the people that statues, religious paintings, stained-glass windows, and side altars should be removed from the churches. He changed the Mass by saying part in Latin and part in German and by giving both the wine and bread to the communicants. This change in the Mass and a few other changes were necessary, but the people were not yet prepared for them. Many therefore were confused and offended. Others were eager to go along with all his extreme ideas.

Matters became worse when some fanatics from Zwickau came to Wittenberg and told the people that they had received a special revelation from the Holy Spirit. Bible reading, they said, was not necessary. God, they said, spoke directly to his people. Infant baptism was wrong. They said that all people have the same rights, no matter whether they are emperors, princes, priests, or peasants, and that education is not desirable or necessary. Unfortunately many of these radical and revolutionary ideas were accepted by some of the people. The result was confusion and disorder in the church and in the city. Riots broke out. Students and citizens interfered with the church services. Altars, statues, windows, and other church furnishings were destroyed. No one seemed to know what to do to bring people to their senses and to restore order. The soft-spoken, timid Melanchthon was helpless. He did not agree with Carlstadt and the other fanatics, but there was little he could do. Spalatin kept Luther informed about these disturbances. Luther was greatly distressed by what was happening. Should he return to Wittenberg to stop Carlstadt and his followers and restore order?

Back to Wittenberg

Elector Frederick was disturbed by the confusion and rioting, but he did not want to do anything that would possibly be contrary to the Word of God. The Wittenberg town council met to decide what should be done. The members soon came to the conclusion that Martin Luther was needed back in Wittenberg. They were convinced that he was the only one to whom the people would listen and the only one who had the leadership ability to restore proper, God-pleasing order. They were sure that the people would respect his judgment. A letter was written and sent to Luther asking him to return to Wittenberg as soon as possible.

When Luther received the letter at the Wartburg, he felt he had no choice. He was needed in Wittenberg. He must go there at once. The elector knew that Luther would be inclined to risk the journey to Wittenberg. He wrote to him and reminded him that he was under the Edict of Worms, and as an outlaw of the state anyone had the right to seize him and kill him. "I advise you," He wrote, "to remain at the Wartburg for the present. If you leave, I cannot give any assurance that I can protect you on the way to or in Wittenberg."

Luther had made up his mind. Still disguised as a knight, he rode out of the Wartburg on March 1, toward Wittenberg, one-hundred-fifty miles away. When he arrived in the town of Borna, he wrote a letter to the elector. In it he stated that he did not expect the elector to protect him. He closed his letter with these words, "I am going to Wittenberg under a far higher protection than that of the elector. I do not intend to ask your Grace's protection. . . . If I thought your Grace could and would defend me by force, I should not come. The sword ought not and cannot decide a matter of this kind. God alone must rule it without human care and operation."

Those brave words written to the elector came from a heart that had complete faith and trust in God. He rode alone and unarmed at the risk of his life. He firmly believed that this is what God wanted him to do and that God would protect him.

X

THE
LEADER

On the evening of March 6, 1522 Luther arrived safely in Wittenberg. As far as he knew, no one had recognized him on the way. At least no one had tried to harm him. God had graciously protected him. He had returned to Wittenberg in defiance of the pope's excommunication and the emperor's ban. He immediately went to the home of his friend Jerome Schurf. Schurf was overcome with joy when he realized that the bearded knight at his door was Martin Luther. The next two days Luther met with Melanchthon, Jonas, and Amsdorf. They discussed the havoc and confusion that had been created by Carlstadt and other trouble-makers. Would Luther be able to bring the people to their senses and restore order?

Preaching and Patience

On Sunday, March 9, Luther again preached from his pulpit in the City Church. This was the first of eight sermons that he preached on successive days. In his sermons he emphasized that not force and regulations can change the hearts of people but only God's Word. He urged all

"All things must be decided on the basis of what God has revealed in his holy Word."

people to be understanding and charitable. He said, "All things are lawful unto me, but all things are not expedient." "All things," he said, "must be decided on the basis of what God has revealed in his holy Word." Luther realized that there were many things in the old church that could not be tolerated. They must be changed or eliminated, but for the sake of peace and harmony these changes should be made gradually. He believed that instruction and patience would bring about the desired, God-pleasing results. In time, peace and quiet were restored. Luther returned to the Black Cloister and resumed his work there as preacher and professor, but many other important matters and responsibilities would occupy much of his time the rest of his life.

The Peasant Revolt

Luther had succeeded in restoring peace in Wittenberg, but radical leaders in other parts of Germany were causing unrest and dissatisfaction among the peasants. In 1524 the peasants revolted against the nobles and princes. The uprising was caused by the injustices that the peasants had to endure. Salaries and other remunerations were usually very inadequate. Housing and living conditions were poor. Although Luther's reformation had to do with the church, the peasants hoped and expected that he would support them in their revolt against their masters. This was a difficult decision for Luther. He was a peasant's son and knew how the nobles and princes often took advantage of the peasants who served them. After much thought, Luther wrote a tract in which he admonished the princes and denounced them for the hardships they were imposing on the peasants by their greed. At the same time, he reminded the peasants that it was wrong to resort to violence. When the peasant uprising under the leadership of Thomas Muenzer developed into an outright war against the nobility, Luther was greatly alarmed. He wrote another tract in which he warned the peasants against rioting and rebellion. He also pointed out that the reformation in which he was involved was not social or political, but religious. Unfortunately Luther's counsel and admonitions went unheeded. The destruction and killings continued for some time before the rebellion was finally put down.

The Authority of God's Word

Germany suffered greatly from this uprising, but the war between peasants and princes also hurt the reformation of the church. Many nobles and peasants felt that Luther had betrayed them. Because they had misunderstood him, they now forsook him. Some rejoined the Catholic Church. Others fell away from the church entirely or joined the Anabaptists. Luther was disheartened. The reformation had suffered a serious setback, but he now also saw his responsibility and task more clearly. He must make his cause and the cause of the Christian church clear, especially to the common people.

Up till now his main aim had been to correct abuses in the old church. He must now, with the blessing of God, help build up the church on earth. The foundation for this building had been laid in his earlier writings. The scriptural principles in those writings needed to be further clarified and applied. God had shown him the right way, and Luther was confident that the Lord would continue to direct him in the tasks that lay ahead. Luther did not consider the work he was doing as his work, but God's work, and therefore he was sure of successs. He wrote, "The cause is God's cause, the care is God's care, the work is God's work, the glory is God's glory. He will conquer also without me, but he has chosen us for his weapon, and we are willing and ready to do his bidding."

Martin Luther realized more than ever that the church and individual Christians needed leadership and guidance based on the authority of God's infallible Word. Through his own experience as a student and monk, he had come to know the influence and power of God's almighty Word. It was God, speaking to him through the Word, who had shown him the right way to eternal salvation. God's Word answered the many questions that had plagued his soul. Once the Word of God became his final authority, he felt secure and was at peace. This the Catholic Church with its pope and misguided bishops and priests had not been able to do. True, they had the Bible, but it was a closed book. They insisted that only the church has the right to interpret the Bible. In fact, the final interpretation, they said, was up to the vicar of Christ, the pope. Luther contended that God gave the Holy Scriptures to all people and that all people have the right to read the Bible and interpret it. He said, "The simple layman armed with the authority of Scripture is to be believed above popes and church councils." When Luther was on trial in Worms, he demanded of his accusers, "Unless you can prove that I am wrong on the basis of Holy Scripture, I cannot and will not recant."

Luther saw that his most urgent task was to get a readable German Bible into the hands of all Christians. He knew and believed that it is only through the Word of God that the Holy Ghost can create faith in the hearts of people and make them members of the Holy Christian Church. The church on earth has no sure foundation unless it is built "upon the apostles and prophets, Jesus Christ being the chief corner stone."

The Translation of the Entire Bible

A number of German translations of the Bible had been made over a period of many years, but they were not accurate and were difficult to understand. They were not made from the original Hebrew and Greek but from the Latin Vulgate Bible, which contained many errors. When Luther translated the New Testament at the Wartburg, he based it on the original Greek text. He completed that translation in the amazingly short time of about three months. The Old Testament required much more time and more intensive work. It meant translating from Hebrew to German. Luther needed help for this arduous task, and he got it from his faithful and gifted co-workers, Melanchthon, Jonas, Bugenhagen, and Amsdorf.

We cannot begin to realize the difficulties Luther and his helpers encountered in making the Hebrew text speak in the language of the common German people. First of all, there was the pressing need to produce a readable German language that most of the common people could comprehend. To accomplish this they went, for example, to the zoo to get the right German names for the animals mentioned in the Bible. From the butcher they learned the right words to be used for the organs in slaughtered animals. They listened to mothers in their homes, to men in the fields, to children in the streets. Luther said, "Sometimes we searched for weeks for a single word and then did not always find it." While working with the Old Testament Prophets Luther exclaimed, "What a huge task it is to make the Hebrew writers speak German! How they balk and will not give up their Hebrew tongue. It is like forcing a nightingale to imitate a cuckoo!"

After twelve years of tireless work, the monumental task was completed. But Luther was never entirely satisfied with the translation — even though it was, and still is, one of the best translations of the Bible ever made. To the very end of his life he was studying the translation and refining it as he compared it with the original Greek and Hebrew. The German translation of the Bible by Luther, with the help of his co-workers, was a masterpiece and a supreme blessing. It gave the German people God's Word in the language that they could understand. And, as a by-product, it gave Germany one literary language. The translation was completed in 1534. By the time of Luther's death in 1546, more than a million copies of the German Bible had been sold.

XI

THE
SCHOOLMAN

When Luther's translation of the New Testament became available in 1522, many people bought copies, but their inadequate skill in reading made it very difficult for them to read and understand God's Word. Luther suspected this. He remembered some of the poor schools he had attended as a schoolboy and the meager instruction he had received in the Word of God.

Efforts To Improve Schools

In 1524 Luther prepared a document titled "An Appeal to the Councilors of the Cities in German Lands to Establish and Maintain Christian Schools." Even today this document is considered one of the most important treatises ever written on the need and importance of good education. In it he wrote: "Dear sirs, must so much money annually be spent for rifles, highways, thoroughfares, dams, and similar countless things in order that a city may enjoy temporal peace and comfort? Why should not at least as much be invested in the needy, poor youth by engaging one or two men as teachers? When one gulden is spent to go to war against the Turks, would it not be better to spend 100 gulden to train one lad to become a true Christian?

"Let us remember the former misery in which we lived! I think that Germany has never before heard so much of God's Word as now. If we permit this to pass by without gratitude and honor, we are in danger of suffering even worse darkness and plague. Beloved Germans, buy while the market is open; gather while the sun shines and the weather is good; make use of God's grace and Word as long as you have it. For this you will know, God's Word and grace are like a fleeting shower, which does not return where once it has been.

"What do we older folk live for if not for the care of the young, to teach and train them? The prosperity of a city does not depend on the accumulation of great riches, the building of walls and houses, many guns and armors. Rather, a city's greatest and best prosperity, salvation, and power is this that it has many fine, learned, sensible, righteous, well-trained Christian citizens."

Elector John, who had succeeded his brother Frederick the Wise as elector of Saxony in 1525, was a staunch supporter of Martin Luther. He suggested to Luther that a thorough investigation be made of the work being done in the schools and churches in Saxony. Luther prepared guidelines for the visitors to help them in carrying out their visitations. He also made some visits himself. The visitations were made in 1528. The visitors inquired about the attitude and conduct of the pastors, about their sermons, about their salaries, about the forms of worship, about the spiritual care received by the lay people, and about the education of the young.

The conditions generally were worse than Luther suspected. He said: "Alas, what manifold misery I beheld! The common people, especially in the villages, know nothing at all of Christian doctrine; and many pastors are quite unfit and incompetent to teach. Yet all are called Christians, have been baptized and enjoy the use of the sacraments;

although they know neither the Lord's Prayer, nor the Creed, nor the Ten Commandments. Still they have, now that the gospel has come, learned to abuse all liberty in a masterly manner. O ye bishops! How will you ever render account to Christ for having so shamefully neglected the people!"

It was very apparent to Luther that some immediate action must be taken. And, even though he was involved with the translation of the Old Testament and many other duties, he went to work to remedy the deplorable conditions. Most of the pastors were former priests and had little knowledge of God's Word. Luther was able to help some by writing sermons for them. Others were dismissed and replaced by more competent and faithful pastors.

Two Catechisms

Luther felt that advising and training parents, teachers, and pastors was not enough. They needed printed materials with which to teach and work. Again, who but Luther himself could undertake the task of producing that material! In 1529 Luther wrote two booklets that are still being used in Lutheran churches and schools throughout the world. They are his two catechisms. He wrote *The Large Catechism*, which he intended for pastors, teachers and adults, first. *The Small Catechism* is familiar to every Lutheran. It was intended for use by parents and small children. In *The Small Catechsim* Luther explains in simple language the main doctines of the Bible. Originally it had five chief parts; the part on the Ministry of the Keys was added later. Both catechisms were thankfully received. *The Small Catechism*, often called the "Children's Bible," was soon found and used in almost every Lutheran home, school and church. In it Luther's faith is clearly and simply expressed. Consider the beautiful explanation of the Second Article:

I believe that Jesus Christ, true God, begotten of the Father from eternity, and also true man, born of the Virgin Mary, is my Lord; who has redeemed me, a lost and condemned creature, purchased and won me from all sin, from death, and from the power of the devil; not with gold or silver, but with his holy, precious blood and with his innocent sufferings and death; that I should be his own, and live under him in his kingdom, and serve him in everlasting righteousness, innocence and blessedness; even as he is risen from death, lives and reigns to all eternity. This is most certainly true.

The Church Service

Through Martin Luther, God had restored the Word of God to the people. They could read it, study it, and hear it. Luther felt that the faith that God had bestowed on the believers through the gospel should be nourished and reflected in the church service. That necessitated changes in the order of the church service. Luther did not, however, go along with the radical changes that Carlstadt advocated. He did not take the view that everything in the old church service must be changed or eliminated. God's Word was his guide. Anything that enhanced the church service should be retained. Anything that was contrary to God's Word should be eliminated or changed.

The Mass was the chief service in the Catholic Church. The ceremony was very elaborate and was conducted in Latin. During the ceremony the priest was thought to have a special power to change the bread and wine into the body and blood of Christ and to repeat Christ's sacrifice on the cross. The lay people were given the bread to eat, but only the priest drank the wine. This, the people were told, was done to avoid spilling any of Christ's blood. The whole ceremony was very mysterious. Most of the Mass was meaningless to the people, but the devout members attended regularly. They believed that going to Mass was a good work that would help save them from eternal damnation. Luther had denounced the Roman Mass as unscriptural in his pamphlet, *The Babylonian Captivity of the Church*. In

1526 he published his *German Mass*. In it he stated that the Lord's Supper should be administered as Jesus instituted it and that the lay people should receive both the bread and the wine. Furthermore, the German language should be used so the people could understand and participate in the service. These changes were wonderful blessings for the people. As they listened and participated, they discovered that the Lord's Supper was not a repetition of the sacrifice of Christ, but a means of grace through which God gave them the forgiveness of their sins.

Luther believed that the pastor's sermon should be the central and important part of the church service. There was preaching in the Catholic Church, but it was secondary to the Mass. The homily, or sermon, was usually poorly done and offered little spiritual benefit to the listeners. Luther contended that the main purpose of every service is to preach and teach the Word of God. Had not Jesus commissioned his disciples to "go and teach all nations" the way to eternal salvation? Luther himself preached several times in a week. His strong faith and deep knowledge of Scripture warmed and stirred hearts of the listeners. He was a powerful preacher. His sermons are still considered models to be imitated. They are scriptural, simple, and down-to-earth, with direct applications to existing situations and problems. The central theme of his sermons always was justification through faith in Jesus Christ. During his lifetime Luther wrote many sermons. More than two thousand are still in existence and have been translated into many languages.

The use of the German language in the church service made possible another change, the singing of the liturgy in German. The liturgy in the Catholic Church was sung or chanted in Latin by the priest and the choir. Luther urged that the German language be used in singing the liturgy and that the congregation be asked to participate. Luther loved singing, and he believed that the singing of religious songs would greatly enhance the church service. In order to have singing in church there must be songs, but the religious songs that were being sung in the homes and elsewhere at that time were not generally suitable for use in church services. Luther again found himself confronted with a task.

XII

THE MUSICIAN
AND POET

Martin Luther loved and appreciated poetry and music. Music was a means of recreation and inspiration for him. To him music was a pleasant diversion from his many arduous duties. He said, "After theology I give the highest honor to music. I would not trade what little I know about music for anything. Next to the Word of God music is the queen of my heart."

Hymns for the Church Service

Luther believed that music, especially singing, was a God-given gift that should serve the gospel. "I am minded," he said, "after the example of the prophets and the fathers of the church to make German psalms for the poeple, that is, spiritual hymns, so the Word of God may be kept among the people through song." He tried to get George Spalatin, Paul Speratus, and others interested in composing religious songs for church services, but they were reluctant. Luther then set himself about the task of producing hymns suitable for congregational singing. In some instances he composed both the poetry and the music.

Luther based his hymns on the Psalms, the early Latin hymns and parts of the church liturgy. His own experience, anguish of heart, and faith are reflected in his hymns. His first attempt at hymnody was inspired by the martyrdom of two young Augustinian students in Brussels in 1523. They were burned at the stake because they refused to renounce their faith. When Luther heard of this he composed a beautiful poem which opened with these lines:

> By help of God I fain would tell
> A new and wondrous story,
> And sing a marvel that befell
> To his great praise and glory.
> At Brussels, in the Netherland,
> He hath his banner lifted
> To show his wonders by the hands
> Of two youths highly gifted
> With rich and heavenly grace.

After describing the martyrdom, the poem closes with this stanza:

> Their ashes never cease to cry,
> The fires are ever flaming.
> The dust thoughout the world doth fly
> Their murd'rers shame proclaiming.
> The voices which with cruel hands
> They put to silence living
> Are heard, though dead, throughout all lands
> Their testimony giving
> And loud hosannas singing.

The first song book for congregational singing appeared in 1524. It consisted of twenty-four hymns. Most of the words had been written by Luther. For some of the hymns he had also composed the music. The people were overjoyed that they could now express their faith and prayers in song. They were eager to learn the words and music and soon

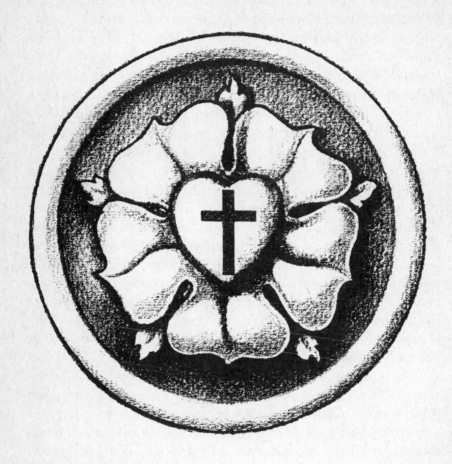

LUTHER'S SEAL: a black cross (mortification) on a white rose (the joy of faith) on a blue field (the joy of heaven) within a golden ring (eternal blessedness).

were singing Luther's hymns not only in church, but in homes, in schools, on the streets, and while working in the fields. The singing of gospel hymns greatly irritated the enemies of the Reformation. At Magdeburg an old weaver was arrested for singing Luther's hymns, "May God Bestow on Us His Grace" and "Out of the Depths I Cry to Thee." When the citizens interceded for him, he was released from jail. The hymns by Luther and others were a powerful means of furthering the cause of the gospel. One Catholic historian wrote: "The songs of Luther have seduced more souls from the Catholic Church than his teaching and preaching."

Luther is truly the father of congregational singing. He made the Lutheran church the singing church. Today hymn-singing is still a very important part of the Lutheran church service, and many of Luther's hymns are still sung by Christians all over the world. Twenty-four of his hymns are found in *The Lutheran Hymnal*. Some favorites are these: Dear Christians, One and All Rejoice; Lord, Keep Us Steadfast in Thy Word; We All Believe in One True God; Come Holy Ghost, God and Lord; From Heaven Above to Earth I Come; and, of course, A Mighty Fortress Is Our God, which is often called "the Battle-Hymn of the Reformation." It is a rugged, powerful hymn. Luther also composed the majestic melody for this hymn, which seems to express better than any other hymn the staunch faith of the great Reformer. In the second stanza of this hymn he says:

> With might of ours can naught be done,
> Soon were our loss effected;
> But for us fights the Valiant One,
> Whom God himself elected.
> Ask ye — who is this?
> Jesus Christ it is,
> Of Sabbaoth Lord,
> And there's none other God;
> He holds the field forever.

THE HUSBAND AND FATHER

Luther occasionally took time out from his work at Wittenberg to visit his parents in Mansfeld. On such visits his father and mother often expressed their concern about his health and well being. His father said to him more than once, "You can't go on the way you are now living. You don't eat nourishing meals regularly, and you don't get the rest you need. You should have someone to look after you and to make a home for you. What you need is a wife. Why don't you get married? You have urged other pastors to do so."

Twelve Helpless Nuns

In 1521 Luther wrote the tract *On the Monastic Vow,* in which he attacked the vow of celibacy and urged monks and nuns to renounce their vows, leave the monasteries and cloisters, and marry. But for various reasons Luther thought it best that he should not marry. He said, "I can't think of marriage for myself. I have too much work and too many responsibilities. I don't have time to look after a household. Furthermore, I am a declared outlaw of the state and can expect the death of a heretic any day. Who would want to marry a man like that?"

A letter received by Luther in the spring of 1523 set in motion a series of events that eventually caused him to change his mind. Many letters and problems came to his attention, and he was always very considerate and patient in giving help and and advice whenever he could, but this request for help was not of the usual kind. It came from a nun in the cloister at Nimbschen, near Grimma. In her letter she stated that she and eleven other nuns wanted to renounce their vows and leave the nunnery, but the abbess would not permit them to do so. If they attempted to leave and were caught, they would be severely punished, possibly with death. Would the good Doctor Luther please help them?

Luther knew that it was a crime punishable by death to aid monks and nuns in their escape from monasteries. But he felt responsible for these nuns who had read his writings and were ready to renounce their monastic vows. He consulted his friend Leonard Koppe. Together they worked out a plan to help the twelve nuns escape. Koppe was a merchant who regularly delivered food supplies to the convent at Nimbschen. One day he delivered a load of herring stored in large wooden barrels. As the nuns unloaded the herring and washed the barrels, he told them of his plan. He said, "After dark watch for your chance to leave the convent. I'll be waiting for you nearby. Climb on my wagon, and then each one of you quickly get into one of the herring barrels. I'll cover the barrels, and we'll be on our way."

The escape was successful. After a few hours' ride Koppe and his wagonload of nuns arrived in Torgau, Koppe's home town. Now there were new problems for the escaped nuns. Where should or could they go? Their relatives and friends may not want to endanger their own safety by befriending escaped nuns. Three did return home, and the rest finally continued on to Wittenberg. They were sure that Luther could somehow help them.

One late afternoon the nine helpless nuns stood in the doorway of the Black Cloister. Luther surmised who they were, but he asked, "Where are you from and why have you come to me?" They said, "We wrote to you for help. Your friend Leonard Koppe helped us escape from the convent in Nimbschen. We thank you, and we hope that you will further help us by finding work for us in Wittenberg."

Luther's problems with the escaped nuns apparently were just beginning. In April 1523 he wrote to his friend, George Spalatin, "Nine fugitive nuns, a wretched crowd, have been brought to me by Leonard Koppe. I pity them much, but most of all I pity the others who are dying everywhere in such large numbers in their accursed, impure celibacy ... O cruel parents and relatives! O pope and bishops, who can curse you enough? Who can sufficiently execrate the blind fury which has taught and enforced such things?

"You ask what I shall do with them? First I shall inform their relatives and ask them to support the girls. If they will not, I shall have the girls provided for. Some families have already promised me to take them in. For some I shall get husbands if I can."

With the help of his associates and townspeople, Luther found work or husbands for all of the girls. Three of the nine remained in Wittenberg. Catherine von Bora found work in the home of the town clerk, Philip Reichenbach, but Luther was not successful in finding a suitable husband for the twenty-six year old Catherine. He tried to arrange a marriage between her and a professor, Dr. Caspar Glatz, but Catherine did not approve of him. When Luther continued his efforts to bring about a marriage between the two, Catherine went to Amsdorf and said, "There are only two men that interest me as husbands, you, Dr. Amsdorf, and Dr. Luther. Please stop Luther from insisting that I marry Dr. Glatz."

Luther was very amused when Amsdorf told him about his conversation with Catherine. Even though Luther approved of and encouraged the marriage of pastors, he still had misgivings about marriage for himself. He still considered marriage undesirable for himself since he daily expected the death of a heretic. Some of his co-workers urged him to marry; others felt that the work of reforming the church would be harmed if he married. His enemies would say that his condemnation of celibacy was motivated by his strong desire to marry. Even Luther's close friend Melanchthon strongly urged him not to marry.

Katie Luther

Martin Luther had learned to know Catherine well. He appreciated her many fine Christian qualities and her abilities. Upon his return to Wittenberg from one of his journeys, he had made up his mind. He wrote to his friend Ruehl, "I have a mind before leaving this world to enter the marriage state, to which I believe God has called me." When he made his proposal of marriage to Catherine, she promptly accepted. The marriage took place in the Black Cloister on June 13, 1525. Only a few close friends were present at the wedding ceremony: Pastor Bugenhagen, who performed the ceremony; Justus Jonas; Lucas Cranach; and Prof. Apel. Catherine von Bora was twenty-six years old at the time, Martin Luther forty-two.

A week later a special church service was conducted in the City Church followed by a wedding feast to which many friends were invited. Luther's aged parents were also present at these two occasions. After the wedding celebration Luther wrote to Amsdorf, "The rumor of my marriage to Catherine is correct. I cannot deny my father the hope of grandchildren, and I had to confirm my teaching that marriage is good and honorable also for pastors."

Catherine, or Katie, as Luther affectionately called her, now became the mistress of the Black Cloister, which the elector of Saxony gave to Luther and his bride as a wedding gift. It was a large, dark, gloomy building with many rooms, corridors, and stairs. But Katie was a good manager, and in time she changed the huge building into a comfortable home. She did everything possible to make life pleasant for her husband. Luther appreciated that his wife was willing to take over the responsibility of changing the cloister into a livable home, because he did not have the time nor inclination to do so.

To her also fell the responsibility of managing the household and the financial problems which arose, especially in the early years of their marriage. She received nothing from her father, who had remarried. Luther's only possessions were his books and clothes. His salary as university professor was barely enough to support him and his wife. Luther's generosity did not help matters any. He said, "I do not worry about debts. When Katie pays one, another one comes along." He was always ready to help anyone who was in need. On one occasion he gave away a beautiful vase that Catherine had received as a wedding gift. This was irritating to Katie. She even found it necessary to hide articles from her husband that were especially precious to her. When Luther received an announcement that their friend Agricola was going to get married, Luther said to Katie, "We should send our good friend a wedding gift. I have in mind sending him that nice goblet that we received as a gift. Where is it? I can't seem to find it."

"Oh, I can't look for it now," Katie replied.

Later that day she said to her husband, "We could have more money, and you would not have to give away our gifts and keepsakes if you would only take some pay for all the things you write and send to the printers. They are making money, and you remain poor."

"Don't worry, my Katie" he replied, "God will take care of us. He always has."

Catherine saw the need for starting a garden. It became the main source of food for the Luther household. In time she also acquired an orchard, a fish pond, chickens, pigs, and several cows. Luther truly appreciated his Katie and helped her with the gardening whenever he could. He said, "I would not change my Katie for all of France and Venice.

She is true to me and a good mother to my children. The greatest happiness is to have a wife to whom you can entrust your business and who is a good mother to your children. Katie, you have a husband who loves you; many an empress is not so well off."

The Luther Home

God blessed the Martin Luther home with six children. Hans was born June 7, 1526. Then followed Elizabeth, Magdalene, Martin, Paul, and Margaret. Elizabeth died in her infancy. The gardener made a wooden cross on which Luther wrote, "Here sleeps Elizabeth, Martin Luther's daughter." She was laid in a grave near the Black Cloister. Luther considered his children precious gifts from a gracious God and loved them affectionately. When Luther's daughter Magdalene was fourteen years old, she became seriously ill. Luther feared that she would not recover. In his grief he bowed to the will of God. As he stood at her bedside he prayed, "Dear Lord, I love my Magdalene very much and I would like to keep her; but dear Lord, if it is your will, take her away. I am glad to know that she will be with you." Then he asked his dying daughter, "Magdalene, would you like to stay here with your parents, or would you willingly go to your Father in heaven?" She answered, "Dear father, I'll do what God wills." On her grave Luther placed this epitaph:

> Here rest I, Luther's daughter, Magdalene,
> With all the saints, upon my bed, serene.
> Although by nature born in sin
> And lost in death I would have been,
> Henceforth I live and have the highest good,
> Eternal life, through Jesus' precious blood.

In spite of hardships and sorrows, the Luther home was a happy and lively one. Luther enjoyed romping and playing with his children. He missed them when he was away on his travels. During his stay at the Coburg Castle in 1530 he wrote a letter to his little son Hans which shows not only his tender love for his boy but also his skill at writing in a way that children can understand and enjoy. A part of that letter follows:

> Grace and peace in Christ, dear little son. I am glad to hear that you are studying and saying your prayers. Continue to do so, my son, and when I come home, I will bring you a pretty present.
>
> I know a lovely pleasant garden where many children are. They wear golden jackets and gather nice apples under the trees, and pears, and cherries, and purple plums and yellow plums. They sing, and run, and jump, and are happy and have pretty little ponies with golden reins and silver saddles. I asked the man who owned the garden who they were. He said, 'They are the children who say their prayers and study and are good.' Then said I, 'Dear man, I also have a son, whose name is Hans Luther; may he come into the garden and eat the sweet apples and pears and ride a fine pony and play with these children?' Then the man said, 'If he says his prayers and is good, he may come into the garden, and Phil and Justy, too; and when they all come, they shall have whistles and drums and fifes and shall dance and shoot little crossbows.' Then he showed me a fine, large lawn in the garden for dancing, where hung real golden whistles and fine silver crossbows. But it was yet early, and the children had not finished eating, and I could not wait to see them dance. So I said to the man, 'My dear sir, I must go and write at once to my dear little Hans about all this, so that he will say his prayers and study and be good, so that he may come into the garden.' So, dear little Hans, study and say your prayers and tell Phil and Justy to say their prayers and study, too, so you may all come into the garden together. God bless you! Give Auntie Lena my love and a kiss from me.
>
> Your loving father,
> Martin Luther

The letter pleased Hans very much, and he had his mother read it to him again and again.

Luther was very much concerned about the education and training that his children received, both at home and in school. He considered child-training the greatest responsibility of parents. He said, "There is nothing which will more surely earn hell for a man than the improper training of children. It is highly necessary that every married person regard the child as a precious, eternal treasure, entrusted to his protection by God so that the devil, the world, and the flesh do not steal and destroy it. On Judgment Day the child will be required from the parents in a very strict reckoning." As can be expected, a Christian atmosphere pervaded the Luther home. Students and visitors were also expected to conform to the established routine and customs. Bible reading, Catechism recitation, prayer, hymn-singing, and family devotions were regular features at various times of the day.

Singing was a happy means of recreation for Luther. After the evening meal he would take his lute and lead the family in singing both secular and sacred songs. Often Jonas, Melanchthon, and other guests and students would join in the singing. The singing of Christian hymns was a source of comfort for him and a means of expressing his faith. He wrote and composed special hymns and carols for simple pageants which he produced for his children at Christmas time. "From Heaven Above to Earth I Come" is such a carol. The first seven stanzas were sung by an older child or a man dressed as an angel. Then the children who were gathered around a cradle with the Baby Jesus responded to the angel's message by singing the remaining stanzas.

The Black Cloister was not limited only to Luther and his family. It was customary at that time for some university students to receive their meals and lodging with their professors. Catherine soon discovered that the big Black Cloister was also a boarding place over which she was the supervisor. Students, relatives, and other guests were constantly coming and going. Some stayed for a meal and the night, others for several days or weeks. When Katie told her husband that she had problems feeding and lodging the many guests who were constantly coming and going, Luther said, "Katie, you seem to forget that it is not you or I who will provide but our heavenly Father. Furthermore, those who travel light travel best.''

The main meal of the day was served in the forenoon at about ten o'clock. That meant that Catherine had to be up early to get the dinner prepared and on the table. Luther liked to tease her by calling her the Morning Star of Wittenberg. Immediately after the meal Luther went to his study. He spent the greater part of the afternoon teaching at the university, preaching, and writing. Evenings he frequently had callers who sought his advice.

Supper was served at five o'clock. After supper, time was often devoted to pleasant and interesting conversation, especially if a good number of students and guests were present. Luther enjoyed exchanging ideas with them and discussing debatable subjects. But when a serious discussion became lengthy and seemed to lag, he would use his good sense of humor to lighten the conversation. He knew that joy and good humor were good medicine to release tensions.

The discussions at the supper table were informal and covered a very wide range of subjects. Luther would lead the discussions, but he always encouraged everyone to ask questions or to make comments. The students and guests greatly appreciated the thoughts that Luther expressed and made a practice of taking notes of his thoughts and observations. These notes were later gathered and published as "Luther's Table Talks." They are interesting and help give us a better understanding of the man Martin Luther. The following are comments taken from Luther's Table Talks:

On the Knowledge of God's Word

A Christian must be well armed, grounded, and furnished with sentences out of God's Word, so he may stand and defend religion and himself against the devil, in case he should be asked to embrace another doctrine.

On the Lord's Prayer

The Lord's Prayer binds the people together, and knits them one to another, so that one prays for another, and together one with another; and it is so strong and powerful that it even drives away the fear of death.

On Serving God

If a man serve not God only, then surely he serves the devil; because no man can serve God, unless he has his word and command. Therefore, if his word and command is not in your heart, you are not serving God, but your own will; for that is upright service to God, when a man does that which God in his Word commands to be done, everyone in his vocation, not that which he thinks good in his own judgment.

On Music

I always loved music; whoever has skill in this art is of a good temperament, fitted for all things. We must teach music in schools; a schoolmaster ought to have skill in music, or I would not regard him; neither should we ordain young men as preachers, unless they have been well exercised in music.

On Death

We must die and suffer death, but whoso holds onto God's Word, shall not feel death, but depart as in a sleep. Whoever finds himself not furnished with God's Word, must die in anguish; therefore, when your time comes to die, make no dispute at all, but from your heart say: I believe in Jesus Christ the Son of God; I ask no more.

At times Luther wrote in fun, serious fun, to help chase away depressing thoughts. He did this by making homey comparisons. One one occasion he had this to say about housewives. "Do you think that the Virgin Mary neglected her housework after Gabriel announced that she would be the mother of the Christ? Not at all. She went home, milked goats, sewed on buttons, scrubbed the floor, and scoured the kettles. Faithful work is honorable before God." Another time Luther said, "Do you think the shepherds who had worshiped the Christ Child went home, shaved their heads, fasted, counted beads, and put on cowls? Never! They returned to their sheep where they were needed."

Martin Luther loved nature, which he called the thousand miracles of God. He enjoyed walking in the nearby woods, grafting fruit trees, tending his rose garden, or helping Katie with the gardening. He enjoyed spying on birds and listening to their singing. One spring two birds had made their nest in a tree near the cloister walk. As he came near the tree they became frightened and flew away. Luther said, "Ah, little bird, do not flee from me. I won't harm you. I'm really your friend. If only you could trust me. But how we are like you! We do not trust our dear Lord God, even though he is good to us and gives us everything we need. He who gave his Son into death for us does not want to harm us. He wants to help us and save us."

Luther's health was not good. Already in his younger years he often complained of severe headaches, indigestion, constipation, heart trouble, ear infections, and other ailments. His poor health, no doubt, was brought about chiefly by the harsh treatment he imposed upon himself as a monk in Erfurt and by the ardor with which he pursued his work. Catherine was greatly concerned about him and did her best to relieve him of household responsibilities and to get him to adopt a routine that was less strenuous. Luther truly appreciated his Katie and what she did for him. He often quoted the passage, "Truly, whoever finds a wife finds a good thing and obtains favor from the Lord." He appreciated his good wife and happy home more and more during the difficult years that lay ahead.

THE DEFENDER OF THE FAITH

XIV

In 1521 Martin Luther stood before the emperor at the Diet of Worms and said, "Unless I be overcome and convinced by proof of the Holy Scriptures . . . , I can and will recant nothing, since it is neither safe nor advisable to do so against conscience." The Catholic Church subsequently declared him a heretic, and the emperor put him under the imperial ban. He was to be taken prisoner and punished with death. But years passed, and the Edict of Worms was not carried out. The emperor knew it would be disastrous for him to antagonize those German princes who supported Luther. The emperor needed their help in his wars with the Turks and with France.

No Longer Alone

In 1521 at Worms Luther stood almost alone and confessed his faith in the truth revealed in the Word of God. In the years that followed, many princes, priests, and lay people became his staunch supporters. The gospel of salvation in Christ was being taught and accepted not only in Germany, but also in the other European countries as well, especially in England, Sweden, Hungary, Holland, and France. All those who accepted the teachings of Luther were called Lutherans. At first the name was used in scorn by his enemies, but Luther's followers were proud to be called Lutherans. Martin Luther objected when people used his name to designate people and churches that were in agreement with him. He said, "I beg you. Use the name Christian, not Lutheran. What is Luther? My teaching is not of my making. It is the teaching of Jesus Christ." We still proudly use the name Lutheran because it means that, just as Luther, we believe that God's holy Word is our only true guide in all matters pertaining to our soul's salvation.

The Marburg Colloquy

Martin Luther firmly believed that the Scriptures are the supreme authority in all matters of faith. He contended that what the Bible says is superior to the pronouncements of popes, the decrees of church councils, or the writings of the church fathers. He also contended that God's Word is superior to human reason. These, however, were not the convictions of some other church leaders who also wanted to reform the church. One such reformer was Ulrich Zwingli.

Zwingli was about the same age as Luther. He lived in Switzerland where he had served as a priest in a Catholic Church for some time. He read many of Luther's writings and was convinced that the Catholic Church was a false church. He began to make changes in the churches he served. He condemned the sale of indulgences and attacked the authority of the pope. He seemed to agree with Luther on the doctrine of justification by faith, but he did not agree with Luther on his interpretation of the Scriptures. Zwingli believed that Scripture must always make sense to human reason. Luther believed that man's reason cannot always fully understand what God says in his Word, but that man must accept in faith what God's Word says.

Philip of Hesse thought that the Reformation could be strengthened if Luther and Zwingli and their followers could unite into one church body. In 1529 he invited Luther, Zwingli and others to meet at his castle in Marburg in order to discuss their doctrinal differences. He thought that differences could be settled through an open and frank colloquy, or discussion. Correspondence between Luther and Zwingli about their doctrinal differences had already been carried on for a long time. There seemed to be agreement on many issues and doctrines.

But a fundamental difference on the interpretation of the Scriptures, especially on how to interpret the words of the Lord's Supper, had not been resolved. Martin Luther and Melanchthon agreed that they and others from Wittenberg should accept the invitation to meet with Zwingli and his supporters at Marburg. But they were determined that no union with the followers of Zwingli could take place unless and until there was complete agreement on every doctrine. They contended that union without doctrinal agreement does not make the church stronger. It weakens it.

The colloquy at Marburg Castle took place in the first days of October, 1529. Luther was the main spokesman for the Lutherans, Zwingli represented the Evangelical Reformers, as the followers of Zwingli were called. In the preliminary meeting several doctrinal matters were discussed, but the main doctrine under consideration was that of the Lord's Supper. Before that discussion began, Luther took a piece of chalk and wrote on the table before him this sentence from the Bible, "This is my body," and covered the writing with a cloth.

Luther contended that the body and blood of Christ are truly present and distributed in the celebrating of the Lord's Supper. He said, "We must take Christ at his word. When Christ said to his disciples, 'Take eat, this is my body,' he meant just that."

Zwingli argued, "How can Christ's body be present here on earth since he is now sitting at the right hand of the Father in heaven? What Christ meant to say was that the bread and wine in the Lord's Supper stand for, or signify, his body and blood."

Luther replied, "Zwingli, you are trampling on God's clear word, just because you cannot explain and understand it." Then Luther removed the cloth from the table, and pointing to the sentence he had written said, "This is what Christ said, 'This *is* my body!' Because Christ said it, I believe it, even though I cannot understand how it is possible. We did not make the sacrament of the Lord's Supper. We merely accept it in faith and thank God for this means of grace."

The discussion continued for three days, but it did no good. Zwingli and his supporters believed that the Lord's Supper was only a memorial celebration of Christ's suffering and death and that the bread and wine were only symbols of Christ's body and blood. Human reason had brought them to that conclusion. They had made reason superior to God's Word.

On the last day of the conference the Lutherans presented fifteen articles to the group, the *Marburg Articles*. Zwingli and his followers agreed to the first fourteen articles. But they rejected the fifteenth, which stated that the true body and blood of Christ were received by those partaking of the Lord's Supper. The hoped-for union did not take place. In spite of the differences between them Zwingli said, "There are no people on earth with whom I should rather unite than with the Wittenbergers." To this Luther replied, "We part in peace, but you have a different spirit from ours."

To accept the false interpretation of Scriptures espoused by Zwingli, Luther would have had to compromise his faith. In doing that he would not have been faithful to God's Word. We thank God that at Marburg Luther was a faithful champion of God's Word and a true defender of the faith.

The Diet of Spires

In 1529 the emperor called for a diet at Spires (Speyer) for the purpose of putting a stop to the Reformation. The major-

of princes, who were Catholic, succeeded in passing resolutions that were harmful to the cause of the Reformation. One resolution stated that Luther's teachings and books should be forbidden in Catholic states, but that Catholic teachings and writings must be permitted in Lutheran states. The evangelical princes objected to this unfair resolution. They protested courageously against its being carried out. They said, "We will never consent to any agreement that will check the preaching and teaching of the gospel in any and all lands. If you do not yield to our request, we protest . . . before God, our only Creator, Preserver, Redeemer, and Savior, who will one day be our Judge." Because they protested, they and other evangelical Christians were called "Protestants." Luther was not at the meeting, but these princes took his place as strong defenders of the faith.

Philip of Hesse felt that the protest at Spires was not enough. He wanted a strong political union of all evangelicals to stand up to the emperor and the Catholic princes. He had hoped that the colloquy at Marburg would result in such a union, but, as we saw, the meeting failed to unite the Lutherans and Reformed. However, the resolution adopted at Spires was not carried out. The preaching of God's Word continued unhindered in bringing more souls to the knowledge of their Savior. "Man proposes, but God disposes!"

The Emperor's Attempt at Reunion

On October 31, 1517 Martin Luther had nailed his *Ninety-five Theses* to the Castle Church door in Wittenberg. That act was his first attempt to reform the Roman Catholic Church. It was not intended as a revolt against the church, and he had no intention of establishing a new church. His one purpose was to bring his church back to the pure teachings of God's Word. In the years that followed, Luther did all within his power to get the pope and other leaders of the Catholic Church to see the errors in their teachings and practices. But he failed in his efforts. They would not concede that Holy Scripture is superior to man-made doctrines and traditions. Instead the church declared Luther a heretic and excommunicated him, and the emperor declared him an outlaw of the state and put him under the imperial ban.

Thirteen years had passed since Luther posted his theses in Wittenberg. Much had taken place since that day. Luther's writings had been distributed throughout Europe. People were again reading their Bibles. The pure Word of God was being preached in many churches and taught in the homes and schools. Many people throughout Europe openly declared that they could no longer support the Catholic Church with its false doctrines and practices.

Emperor Charles V felt that these conditions could not be tolerated. As a good Catholic, he believed the true Christian church was the visible Catholic Church. Therefore he wanted all Christians to settle their differences and return to the "Mother Church." He thought that it would be a simple matter to restore peace and to reunite the church if the issues that divided the Christians could be clearly outlined and frankly discussed.

In January 1530 Charles V announced that a diet would be held at Augsburg, Germany, beginning on April 8. At that diet, over which Charles V himself would preside, the differences that divided the church were to be presented and hopefully resolved. When Elector John of Saxony received the announcement, he immediately ordered Luther and his co-workers to prepare a document that would clearly set forth the main teachings and practices of the Lutherans. Luther, Melanchthon, Bugenhagen , and Justus Jonas prepared several brief articles in which they set forth the basic Lutheran teachings as they were drawn from the the Scriptures. These articles would be revised several times before they wold be presented at the diet.

On April 3 Luther, Melanchthon, Jonas, Spalatin, Agricola, and Elector John left for Augsburg. After a twelve-day journey, they arrived in Coburg. There they were informed that the emperor would be late in getting to Augsburg and that the opening of the diet would be delayed. Finally, on April 22, Elector John received word that the emperor would arrive in Augsburg at the end of the month. The next morning the elector and his companions set out for Augsburg. The elector did not permit Luther to go on with them to Augsburg since he still was under the imperial ban. Luther was very disappointed at the thought of being separated from his friends by one-hundred-thirty miles during those crucial days. But he still hoped that he would be asked to come later. It was now primarily up to Melanchthon to take Luther's place at the diet as the defender of the faith. This was a great responsiblity and burden for a man who frequently had not displayed the leadership that would now be required of him. He was inclined to be timid and conciliatory. Yet he was a man with many gifts, and Luther greatly admired him.

The Leader on Coburg

The Diet of Augsburg dragged on for five months. During that time Luther was confined to the Castle Coburg. There he was safe, yet near enough to Augsburg so that Melanchthon and others could communicate with him about the proceedings at the diet. He occupied himself very profitably with reading and writing, but his thoughts and prayers were almost constantly with his friends in Augsburg. Once he wrote to Melanchthon, "Dear Philip, we have at last reached our Sinai, but we will make a Zion of this Sinai. This is a very attractive place, and just made for study. Only your absence grieves me. I shall pray and cry to God to bless our cause and not stop till my cry is heard in heaven."

He mentioned several writing projects that he had in mind. One was called an *Admonition to the Clergy Assembled at the Diet at Augsburg*. This tract was printed in May. In it Luther reminded the Catholic leaders of the falsehoods that had been forced upon the people and warned them to desist lest they bring about a rebellion. He also promised that if they would let the gospel have free course, their properties and possessions would not be disturbed. Luther's chief work at the Coburg was the continuation of the translation of the Bible into German. He also wrote commentaries on several psalms. Besides his self-assigned work, he carried on constant correspondence with his co-workers in Augsburg, especially with Philip Melanchthon. He also wrote regularly to his wife, who worried a great deal about him and about the outcome of the diet.

In one of his letters Luther wrote, "Brother Philip, your many cares and worries are consuming your energy. You and I know that our cause is great and our Champion Jesus Christ is also great. He will give us the victory. What good can all the worry do you? What more can the devil do than kill us? I beg you to fight against yourself, your own worst enemy. Jesus Christ who died for us lives and reigns. He is on our side. I pray God to increase your faith and the faith of all people. If we have faith in our Savior, neither the devil nor the world can harm us." It was from the Coburg Castle that Luther sent his well-known letter to his four-year-old son Hans.

Luther's stay at the Coburg was much more pleasant in some ways than his forced exile at the Wartburg. He appreciated the comfortable quarters, good food, companionship and beautiful surroundings, but he missed his family and longed to be with his friends at the diet in Augsburg. His health was not good. His old ailments gave him much discomfort and made him very weak. Sometimes he could not do any work for days at a time. He wrote to Melanchthon, "Dear friend, I cannot write at length. My headache is so severe that I cannot read your letter with proper understanding. I can hardly bear to open my eyes and look at the light." On June 5 Luther received the sad news that his aged father had died on May 29. This grieved him very much. After he had read the letter, he said to his companion Veit Dietrich, "So, then, my father too is dead." Then he took his prayer book and went to his room. After he had given vent to his tears, he thanked God for the many blessings he had granted him through his father.

The correspondence between Coburg and Augsburg increased when Melanchthon found it necessary to rewrite and enlarge parts of the confessional document. When the final copy was completed, it was sent to the Coburg Castle for Luther's approval. After reading it, Luther worte, "I am well pleased with it and cannot see how I could improve or change it; nor would it be proper for me to attempt it, for I cannot step so softly and gently. Christ, our Lord, grant that it may become a great blessing for all Christendom. That is my hope and prayer."

After much delay, the emperor finally arrived in Augsburg. On the evening of June 15 Charles V summoned the evangelical princes and told them to forbid the Lutheran ministers who had come to Augsburg to preach the gospel in the city. Several princes told the emperor that he could not dictate to their conscience. Margrave George exclaimed, "Before I would deny my God and his gospel, I would rather kneel down before your imperial majesty and let you cut off my head." That unexpected remark shocked the emperor. In his broken German he stammered, "Not the head off! Not the head off!" Then he dismissed the princes. When Emperor Charles asked everyone to participate in the traditional Corpus Christi procession, the Lutheran princes refused.

The Augsburg Confession

After several preliminary meetings and many delays, the emperor set June 25 as the day for the presentation of the Lutheran document. The document, which would be known as the *Augsburg Confession*, consisted of 28 articles. It was written in both German and Latin. All the Lutheran princes who were at Augsburg signed the document, even though they knew that they could be put under the imperial ban as Luther had been. The Prince of Anhalt expressed the conviction of all the signers when he said, "I would rather quit the country of my father, staff in hand, rather gain my bread by cleaning the shoes of foreigners, than receive any other doctrine than that contained in this confession."

The reading of the *Augsburg Confession* took place on the afternoon of June 25, 1530, a date to be remembered in the history of the Lutheran Church. The small chapel was crowded to capacity. Those who could not get into the chapel stood outdoors and listened at the open windows. It was agreed that the German copy of the confession be read. At three o'clock Dr. Christian Beyer, Chancellor of Electoral Saxony, stepped forward and began to read in a loud, clear voice. Everyone in the room and outside near the windows could hear him. The reading took two hours, but everyone listened with close attention. The Latin and German copies of the confession were then given to the imperial secretary.

The reaction to the Lutheran confession varied. Some Catholic princes condemned the confession as being heretical. Others admitted that they had been misinformed concerning the Lutheran teachings and thought that the confession was correct in most parts. Duke William said to Dr. Eck, "It is the truth, the pure truth. We cannot deny it. What are you going to do to refute it?" To this Eck is supposed to have replied, "I can refute it from the church fathers, but on the basis of Scripture I cannot refute it." The duke then asked Eck, "Do I understand you to mean that the Lutherans are sitting in the Scriptures and we on the outside?" The confessional articles of the Lutherans clearly proved that it was the Roman Catholic Church, not the Lutheran Church, which had forsaken the Bible and the true teaching of Christianity. It should be mentioned that officials of some free cities also signed their names to the confession soon after it was read.

Martin Luther rejoiced when he heard that the confession had been read publicly and that his elector and co-workers had boldly professed their faith before the world. He wrote to Elector John: "I thank God that I lived to see this hour.

Christ was with us. The reading of the confession at the diet has done more good than the sermons of ten doctors."

The *Augsburg Confession* had clearly stated the doctrinal position of the Lutherans. The next move was up to the emperor. He at once directed two Catholic theologians, Eck and Cochlaeus, to prepare a refutation of the *Augsburg Confession*. That document, called the *Confutation*, was completed on August 3. Many lengthy negotiations were now carried on between those who supported the Lutheran document and those who condemned it. The emperor was still hopeful that a satisfactory solution could be reached at the diet so that the Lutherans would return to the "Mother Church." It was very clear to Luther, however, that an agreement on doctrine was out of the question. He could not understand why his co-workers and the Lutheran princes continued the useless negotiation with the Roman Catholics. But Melanchthon was hopeful, and in his weakness was even willing to make some concessions. This greatly troubled Luther. A steady stream of letters came from Luther to Melanchthon and others. He rebuked them for trying to compromise Scriptural truths and encouraged them to remain steadfast.

When the emperor realized that little progress was being made, he gave his final verdict on September 22. He declared that the *Augsburg Confession* had been effectively refuted by the *Confutation* prepared by the Catholic clergy. The Lutheran princes, provinces, and cities would have until April 15, 1531 to return to the Catholic Church. After that date force might be used to make them yield. During that time the Lutherans were not to publish and make available any new books on religion. Nor were they to make any attempts to induce any subject of the emperor to accept the Lutheran faith. The decree was to remain in force until the emperor would arrange for a general council meeting.

The Lutherans of the diet objected strenuously to the statement of the emperor that Eck's *Confutation* had effectively refuted the *Augsburg Confession*. Melanchthon immediately set to work to prepare a response to the emperor's statement. Melanchthon's response is known as the *Apology of the Augsburg Confession*. "Apology" here means defense. When the *Apology* was presented on September 22, the emperor refused to receive it. That ended the possibility of any further debate. The princes and theologians then left for their respective homes. On the way home Elector John stopped at the Castle Coburg for a visit with Luther. Together they went on to Torgau, where Luther preached on Sunday. Luther then continued on to Wittenberg for a long awaited reunion with his family. He had been away for more than six months.

The Diet of Augsburg had not resolved the religious differences between the Lutherans and the Catholics. Rather, it served to unite the Lutherans. In Augsburg they had publicly declared their agreement in doctrine when they adopted and supported the *Augsburg Confession*. They came away from Augsburg stronger in faith and more determined than ever that no one would take from them the truth of the gospel that God had restored to them through Reformation.

The Smalkald League and Articles

The emperor's decree and threat at the diet also drove the Protestants to form a union. The princes felt they should be prepared to defend themselves if and when the emperor would attempt to carry out his decree. In 1531 an alliance of Lutheran princes, states, and cities was formed at Smalkald known as the Smalkald League. As it gained more members it became a formidable power with which the emperor would have to reckon should he decide to use force to carry out his decree against the Protestants.

The emperor had given the Lutherans until April 15, 1531 to consider whether or not they would renounce the *Augsburg Confession* and return to the Catholic Church. When the time came for their reply, none was made. The emperor did nothing about it. He was too busy fighting the Turks to be bothered with the Lutherans in Germany. But he had not forgotten his promise to arrange a general council meeting to settle the matters that were dividing the Lutherans and Catholics. He was still hopeful that a reunion could be accomplished. He persuaded the pope to summon a general council meeting at Mantua in June. The Protestants were asked to send delegates to the meeting.

Elector John was opposed to such a council because he well knew that the purpose of the council was to condemn and, finally, destroy the Lutherans. Luther was of the same opinion. After consulting with the members of the Smalkald League, it was decided that Luther should draw up articles of confession that would be presented at the council meeting. Luther gladly consented to prepare such a document. He never had been completely satisfied with the *Augsburg Confession* and its *Apology*. They were good as far as they went, but he felt that Melanchthon did not speak out strongly enough against the false teachings of the Catholic Church. In some instances he did not state clearly the differences in doctrines between the two church bodies. Some differences had not even been mentioned. Luther appreciated this opportunity to prepare a comprehensive document in which he could officially testify to his faith and teachings. By Christmas 1536 the twenty-two articles were completed. Elector John was very pleased with them and told Luther that he was ready to defend them before the general council. They were signed by the leading theologians in Wittenberg and became known as the *Smalkald Articles*. This confession is one of the great confessional documents of our Lutheran Church.

Elector John now asked a number of theologians and princes to meet with him in Smalkald to make further preparations for the general council meeting. Luther, Bugenhagen, and Melanchthon went with him. Several days after they arrived, Luther became very ill and begged that he be taken home to Wittenberg. He suffered agonizing pains from kidney stones. The ride over rough roads was ex-

tremely painful to him. He thought his end was near. On the
way he made his last will and received the Lord's Supper
from his pastor, John Bugenhagen. Once when his pain
temporarily subsided he wrote to his wife, "I was dead and
had commended you and the children to God, but God did
miracles on me this night, and is still doing them, because
of the intercession of faithful men." Finally, on March 14,
he arrived home, but his recovery was very slow and left
him in a weakened condition for several weeks.

Meanwhile Elector John and his advisors decided to
decline the invitation to attend the general council meeting.
They gave these reasons: The council planned for Mantua
would not be a free Christian council since the decisions
had already been made by the Catholics. The Lutheran
states would not have equal representation. The basis of
judgment would not be the Bible, but the human judgment
of the pope. The meeting would not take place in Germany.
That ended the possiblity of a council meeting.

Luther's articles were not presented. He, however, hoped
that they could be presented at some future meeting. In 1538
he edited them very carefully and had them published.
They were widely distributed and soon were looked upon as
presenting the official doctrinal position of the Lutheran
Church together with such confessional documents as
Luther's catechisms, the *Augsburg Confession*, the *Apology of the Augsburg Confession,* and the writing Melanchthon presented at the Smalkald meeting, *Of the Power and Primacy of the Pope.*

In all these diets, controversies, and meetings, Martin
Luther stands out as the staunch confessor of the true faith.
He firmly believed that God's Word is infallible and that
justification by faith in Christ is the central teaching of the
Bible. He insisted that human reason must subject itself to
the truths that God reveals in his Word. Therefore Luther
would not compromise with Carlstadt, Zwingli, and others
who subjected God's Word to their reason. He believed that
the strength of the church on earth lay not in size or out-

ward organization. He disagreed with Melanchthon's compromising efforts and with Philip of Hesse's attempts at union without full doctrinal agreement. Luther's faith filled him with courage and strength to profess the truth in spite of threats from emperors and pope, and caused him to exclaim:

> The Word they still shall let remain
> Nor any thanks have for it;
> He's by our side upon the plain
> With his good gifts and Spirit.
> And take they our life,
> Goods, fame, child, and wife,
> Let these all be gone,
> They yet have nothing won;
> The Kingdom ours remaineth.

XV

THE DEATH
OF THE FAITHFUL BELIEVER

Martin Luther's last years on earth were difficult for him. He was weary from his arduous labors, and his body was wracked with pain. It grieved him that some of his co-workers were at times willing to compromise scriptural truths in order to maintain peace and unity. He was worried about a possible civil war in Germany. The immoral conditions in Wittenberg and lack of discipline among the students at the university troubled him. But he never lost his trust in God and his Word. As he looked back on his years of labor, his heart was filled with thanksgiving. Where formerly only a few had been able to find the true way to eternal salvation, many now knew and believed the gospel that a man is justified by faith in Christ Jesus. In 1542 Luther wrote: "To me, a poor, unworthy, miserable sinner, God the Father of mercy, has entrusted the gospel of his dear Son and has kept me true and faithful therein. As a result, many in the world have received the gospel and hold me to be a true teacher — despite pope, emperors, kings, princes, priests, and all the devil's wrath."

God's Faithful Servant

Luther bore his sufferings patiently, and despite his poor health, continued to carry out his regular duties. He even became involved in more writing and speaking. A month before his death he wrote humorously: "Old, decrepit, sluggish, weary, worn out, I write to you. Now that I am dead —as I seem to myself — I expect the rest I have deserved to be given me, but instead I am overwhelmed with writing, speaking, doing, transacting business, just as though I had never done, written, said, or accomplished anything."

In late summer 1545 he tried to get relief for his body and mind by taking a journey with his friend Caspar Cruciger. It was intended to be a pleasure trip, but at Zeitz Luther was asked to take part in settling a dispute that had arisen betwen two pastors. At Merseburg he was prevailed upon to consecrate Prince George of Anhalt as administrator. He also preached several times during the journey. After several weeks Luther and Cruciger returned to Wittenberg. On November 10 he celebrated his birthday for the last time with his family and his close friends, Melanchthon, Bugenhagen, Cruciger, and Ebert. The celebration was jovial, but the thought of death kept coming to Luther's mind. He told his companions at the gathering that he longed for the time when God would graciously relieve him of his sufferings and take him to his heavenly home.

A week later he completed his lectures at the university on the Book of Genesis. At the close of the last lecture he said to the students, 'There, that is the good Book of Genesis. I can do no more. I am weak. God grant me a blessed end!'"

The Last Journey

Early in January 1546 Luther was asked to come to Eisleben to help settle a bitter dispute that had developed between the counts of Mansfeld. The journey was made in an open carriage in bitter cold weather. Justus Jonas and Luther's sons, Hans, Martin, and Paul, went with him.

"Father, into your hands I commend my spirit."

He wrote often to his wife when absent from home, because he knew that she was greatly concerned about his health. His letters always were cheerful, and he expressed the hope that the quarrel between the counts could be settled speedily and that he and the boys could soon return. He wrote his last letter to her on February 14: "Dear Katie, we hope to come home this week if God wills . . . Your sons are still at Mansfeld. James Luther takes care of them. We eat and drink like lords, and they wait on us so well — too well, indeed, for they might make me forget you in Wittenberg. Moreover, I am no more troubled with the stones. God bless you!"

God's Faithful Servant Taken Home

On February 17 the final agreement was reached between the counts. On that day Luther preached his last sermon. That evening he suddenly complained of faintness and pressure on his chest. Jonas and Luther's sons, who had returned from Mansfeld, became alarmed. The doctor was called and gave him some medicine. Luther retired at eight o'clock, but awoke again at ten. The pain had not subsided. To Jonas he said, "I was born and baptized here in Eisleben. This is where I may die." He lay down on a couch and fell asleep. At two o'clock he awoke suffering from intense pain in the chest. He raised himself up and prayed, "Into your hands I commit my spirit. You have redeemed me, O God of truth." He knew that death was near. He continued praying: "O my heavenly Father, I thank you that you have given me your Son Jesus Christ, in whom I believe, whom I have preached and confessed, loved and praised, whom the wicked pope and the godless shame, persecute and blaspheme. I pray you, dear Lord Jesus Christ, let me commend my soul to you. I am certain that I shall be with you forever and that no one can ever tear me out your hands. Father, into your hands I commend my spirit. You have redeemed me. Amen." Luther fell back exhausted and closed his eyes. Jonas shook him and spoke in a loud voice, "Reverend Father, are you ready to die in the faith of your Lord Jesus Christ and in the doctrine which you preached in his name?"

"Yes," whispered Dr. Luther. The Lord Jesus took the soul of his servant to its heavenly home. The life of the great Reformer and faithful believer had come to an end. He was sixty-two years old when he died on February 18, 1546.

God's Faithful Servant Laid To Rest

The next afternoon a memorial service was conducted in St. Andrew's Church in Eisleben. Justus Jonas preached the sermon. He compared Luther with Moses who had led the Children of Israel out of slavery to the Promised Land. The following morning Michael Coelius preached another sermon in the same church. The funeral procession left for Wittenberg. A troop of the cavalry rode in front of the procession. On February 22 Luther's body arrived in Wittenberg where many people were waiting to join the procession to the Castle Church. Luther's widow, his three sons, and relatives followed in carriages behind the wagon that carried the body of Luther. Then came nobles, princes, city officials, students, professors, and many other mourners. The casket was carried to the front of the church. As many people as possible crowded into the church to pay their respects. Luther's pastor and close friend, John Bugenhagen, preached the funeral sermon. He spoke about Luther's work and how God blessed his labors in his lifetime. Philip Melanchthon spoke for the university. He called Luther the greatest religious leader and theologian since St. Paul. After the service Luther's body was lowered into a grave at the front of the pulpit. His body was laid to rest in the church were he posted his *Ninety-five Theses* in 1517 and where he had preached many of his sermons.

The great leader of the Reformation was dead. Many throughout Europe mourned his death. His family, friends, and fellow-workers felt the loss most keenly. Luther's co-worker and close friend, Philip Melanchthon, exclaimed,

"Alas! passed away is the charioteer and chariot of Israel who has guided the church in this period of the world. It is not human wisdom that has discovered the doctrine of the forgiveness of sins and trust in the Son of God, but God has revealed it through this man, whom God himself called forth, as we have seen. May we therefore love this man's memory and the doctrine which he taught, and let us be humble and consider the great tribulations and changes which will follow his death. O Son of God, I pray you to rule, maintain and protect your church on earth!"

XVI

OUR HERITAGE

For many years the true way to eternal salvation had been hidden by misbelief, traditions, and man-made doctrines. Through the study of the Holy Scriptures God led Martin Luther to recognize the soul-destroying errors that were being preached and taught. God led him to believe that the only way to eternal salvation is through justifying faith in Christ Jesus. The discovery of this glorious truth of the Bible brought peace and joy to his soul. But he could not keep the good news of salvation to himself. He made it his life's work to dispel the darkness of misbelief and to restore the gospel to the world. After more than four-hundred years we still have that gospel in its truth and purity. That is our Reformation heritage.

Luther's first and foremost task was to make God's Word, the Bible, available in the language that the German people could read and understand. This was a twelve-year undertaking. As a result, the people could read for themselves what God has to say to them in his Word. That was the beginning of making God's Word available to people all over the world. Bible portions are now printed in more than fifteen-hundred languages. Through Luther, God brought it about that we today are also able to read the Bible in our own language. That is our Reformation heritage.

Martin Luther felt that the chief doctrines of the Bible should be known well by every Christian. He therefore prepared two books that would help adults and children learn and understand the basic teachings of God's Word. Those two books, the *Large* and *Small Catechisms*, have become the textbooks in Christianity for millions of people throughout the world. Today we still have Luther's catechisms — an important part of our Reformation heritage.

Luther believed that the congregation should participate more fully in the church service. He suggested that hymn-singing by the congregation be made an important part of the service. He encouraged the writing of appropriate hymns and wrote thirty-six himself. Through Luther's effort and encouragement, God has given us many gospel hymns and the joy of singing them in our church services and elsewhere. That is our Reformation heritage.

Luther was very much concerned about the education of children and young people. He felt that the welfare of the state and church depended on good schools. Together with Melanchthon he drew up plans for primary and secondary schools. His concerns and opinions on education are still our concerns and thoughts today. That is why we establish and maintain Christian schools where children can be brought up in the nurture and admonition of the Lord. That is our Reformation heritage.

Luther's faith was grounded solely on God's Word. He boldly confessed that faith in his sermons, in his debates, and in his many articles and letters. We see this Bible-based faith in the *Augsburg Confession*, the *Apology of the Augsburg Confession*, and the *Smalkald Articles*. These three confessions, together with Luther's *Large* and *Small Catechisms* and the *Formula of Concord*, were published in one book in 1580 called the *Book of Concord*. All the confessional writings and every statement in these writings are

based on the truth found in the Word of God and as taught
and believed by Dr. Martin Luther. They are our Reformation heritage.

129

O God, our Lord, thy holy Word
Was long a hidden treasure
Till to its place it was by grace
Restored in fullest measure.
For this today our thanks we say
And gladly glorify thee.
Thy mercy show and grace bestow
On all who still deny thee.

Salvation free by faith in thee,
That is thy gospel's preaching
The heart and core of Bible-lore
In all its sacred teaching.
In Christ we must put all our trust,
Not in our deeds of labor;
With conscience pure, a heart secure,
Love thee, Lord, and our neighbor.

Thou, Lord, alone this work hast done
By thy free grace and favor
All who believe will grace receive
Through Jesus Christ, our Savior.
And though the Foe would overthrow
Thy Word with grim endeavor,
All he has wrought must come to naught —
Thy Word will stand forever.

— Martin Luther, 1527